JOSHUA'S DREAM

A Town with Two Names

A Story of Old Southport
by
SUSAN S. CARSON

For Richard and Esperanza Pravatte, with lots of good wishes. Susan Carson 12-12-92

A birthday gift for my town and its people in
Southport's bicentennial year of 1992

First Edition

Photo Credit: *The State Port Pilot*
New Hanover County Library

Published by Carolina Power and Light Company
Southport, North Carolina

Printed in the United States of America
by
Wilmington Printing Company
Wilmington, North Carolina

For My Daughter,

KATHRYN ELIZABETH CARSON

*who made me believe I could write this book and
who encouraged and helped me all the way*

and

In Memory of My Father,

CRAVEN LEDREW SELLERS (1889-1960)

who kindled in me a love for local history

Foreword

Susan Sellers Carson was born in 1920 in Supply, North Carolina, the oldest of three children born to Ledrew Sellers and his wife, Lelia Sellers Sellers. She descended from the early Sellers and Hewett families of Brunswick County, predating the American Revolution. Moving with her family to Southport at the age of two, "Miss Susie" has lived here all of her life except for a year of early married life in Virginia.

As valedictorian, Susan Carson graduated from Southport High School in 1937. After taking business courses and extra social studies classes at Shallotte High School in 1939, she began her career as a legal secretary in Southport in 1940, putting herself in a position to observe firsthand a goodly portion of recent Southport history.

A longtime member of the Southport Baptist Church, Susan Carson serves her church in many ways—Sunday school teacher, librarian, archivist, historian, editor, choir member, and deacon, among many others. Community activities that are especially important to her are charter membership and past presidency of the Southport Historical Society, and trustee of the Brunswick County library for over twenty years. "Miss Susie" currently is editor of the history page in *Whittlers Bench*, the newsletter of the Southport Historical Society. In addition she is a member of the Brunswick County Historical Society, Old New Hanover Genealogical Society, and the North Carolina Genealogical Society.

Susan Carson is the author of *By Faith We Serve*, a history of Southport Baptist Church from 1871 to 1991, and *Song of Remembrance*, a history of the Woman's Missionary Union of the Brunswick Baptist Association from 1902 to present. Today she is the editor of a Baptist Women's newsletter, *Baptist Women News & Views*.

Joshua's Dream was written because of Susie Carson's love of Southport which is second only to her love of her church. Her passion for the Southport story has continued to increase since she was requested, in 1983, to consolidate her research to teach a course on local history at the Brunswick Community College Southport Campus. She has said many times that she "didn't think many folks would be interested enough in what she might say to sit through weeks of lectures." Boy, was she wrong. Her classes fill and often second classes are added each quarter she teaches. Over the past nine years the lesson plans for these classes evolved into outlines for chapters of a book on the history of Southport. The publishing of this book became "Miss Susie's Dream." Carolina Power and Light Company is proud to publish Susan Carson's manuscript, *Joshua's Dream*, for Southport's Bicentennial Celebration.

Vicki Spencer

Carolina Power and Light Company   Editor

Table of Contents

Acknowledgments

If I could attempt to acknowledge the names of everyone who has contributed to this book, then I would simply have to write another book for acknowledgments only. However, I must try to list some who have contributed in unique and special ways. To those I have not named or could not remember, I am also forever grateful.

Bill Reaves, without whose research and other help, I could not have written this book. As my dear friend Dorothy Potter Munson said about Bill: "He is a treasure."

Kathryn Carson, my daughter, inspired me to write and shared her Brunswick Town, Southport, and Wilmington research with me. She also enlarged my library with reference books and gave me much needed office supplies.

Stephen Dunn, my nephew, shared invaluable research on the Civil War and World War II, and also contributed greatly to my store of needed office supplies.

Francey C. Wertz, friend and advisor, helped with research and transportation. She also counseled me, gave encouragement when I might have given up, and listened to my many lengthy discourses about *Joshua's Dream*.

David Kelly and Vicki Spencer of Carolina Power and Light Company patiently guided this book through press and offered many words of reassurance.

Elaine LeGrand fed the manuscript into the computer, made many needed corrections, and gave me confidence when I needed it most.

Mary L. McKeithan answered so many questions about bygone years in Southport.

Donna E. Crocker, my friend and helper, furnished transportation for many trips to the library for research and ran errands for me while I was in the throes of writing and re-writing.

Thelma S. Dunn, my sister, shared her memories and her scrapbook of growing up in Southport; and her husband Bill ran errands, performed chores, and listened cheerfully as I told this story many times in my history classes.

Mr. and Mrs. James M. Harper, Jr., have done so much to preserve the town's heritage.

Others who have been so very helpful are Cassie S. Cockran, Mary Shannon, Eula Mae Franck, Christopher Suiter, Carl Lounsbury, Lena W. Fisher, Beverly Tetterton, Lucy A. Avant, Carl E. Swain, Ronald Gooding, Frances Reilly (now deceased), James D. Ward, Sylvia Butterworth, Stuart Callari, Elnora H. Rogers, Cheryl R. Daniel, Sally McNeil, Trudy Hufham, Hazel Willetts, Edward Jelks, and last, but not least, all my students who so willingly listened to my lectures, made suggestions, and urged me on.

Preface

Information for this story of Southport has been gathered over a period of many years and from many sources. I cannot begin to remember all the books I have read and studied and all the materials I have sifted through in my quest for information on how Smithville/Southport came to be. I collected hundreds of newspaper and magazine articles; there were diaries, court minutes, census records, letters, unpublished manuscripts, church records, personal interviews, and pamphlets from which I gleaned bits and pieces of the town's history; and, of course, there were also my own memories of living in Southport from my very early childhood.

Miss Annie May Woodside (1892-1981), who was born and lived in Southport all her life, was my mentor and special friend. She often asked me to write a history of Southport and gave me many items for it. In our conversations she made old Southport so real to me that I felt I was living in that time.

The materials I gathered were stored in file cabinets, boxes, notebooks, and pamphlet boxes on my library shelves and in the closets of my home. I simply could not resist any scrap of material that in any way related to Southport. Indeed, there were times that all I found were scraps of paper with no date or source given. I didn't know just what I would do with my collection; I just knew I would never throw it away.

About ten years ago, at the urging of friends and newcomers to Southport who wanted to know more of its history, I began teaching local history at Brunswick Community College's Southport campus. Many requests came from organizations to speak on local history. From these two experiences I came to realize there was a need for a narrative of Southport's history. We already had the excellent two-volume *Southport Chronology* by Bill Reaves, but Southport's history had never been told in narrative form. Encouraged by my daughter and students, I came to the decision to put my lecture notes into a book to bring together the story of old Southport.

Then came the request from David Kelly, Manager of External Relations at Carolina Power and Light Company and Chairman of the Board of Trustees of Brunswick Community College, that I write and allow CP&L to publish a book on Southport's history. The book would be a part of the company's contribution to Southport's bicentennial celebration. I was delighted, of course, to accept his offer. I extend my thanks to Mr. Kelly and to CP&L for making the publication possible. It has been a special privilege to work with David Kelly and Vicki Spencer, both of CP&L, in the preparation of this manuscript.

My sincere hope is that *Joshua's Dream* will tell the story of this "Town With Two Names" and that it will serve as a textbook for future teachers of our local history.

The book is not meant to be a scholarly treatise but rather an authentic story of the town I love. I have made no attempt to include footnotes for every statement made. The sources used are listed in the *Bibliography and Suggested Reading List*. Sources of exact quotations are given in the text itself.

It has been a joy to write this book. As I have moved back in time I have relived every scene. For those who have always known and loved Southport, I hope it will kindle memories and renew your devotion; and to those who have just lately come to live among us, I hope it will help you know how Southport came to be the town it is today.

Susan S. Carson
Southport, N. C.
November 1992

Prologue –
Early Quest of the Cape Fear Region

In his book, *The Lower Cape Fear in Colonial Days*, Dr. Lawrence Lee, eminent historian and author, says:

> *In the world in which we live, the Lower Cape Fear is but a minute part. In its narrow sense its history is parochial. In a broader sense, however, it is a case study of the founding, development, and eventual freedom of a British possession. And because the region conformed so well to the English mercantile system, it was a classic example of the role the mother country expected her possessions to play. In that perspective the history is an integral part of the story of the British empire during the 18th century. It is also an important chapter in the creation of a mighty nation, the United States of America.*

With Dr. Lee's words in mind, we look then at the period of early explorations and settlements along the North Carolina coast near the mouth of the Cape Fear River. At one time or another, Spain, France, and England each laid claim to the lower Cape Fear area. This section is loosely defined as the region that lies near the lower reaches of the Cape Fear River and its tributaries or the area extending outward to a perimeter of fifty miles beyond the conjunction of the river and its Northeast Branch. To claim the land was one thing; to possess it, however, is an entirely different matter.

Five years after the discovery of the New World by Columbus, two sea captains sailing for England also found America, and their discovery became the basis for England's right to settle the New World. England, just then emerging from the long conflict known as the *War of Roses*, was drained of strength and had no interest in colonizing America. The claim was to lie dormant for more than a hundred years.

The year 1524 brought Giovanni da Verrazano, an Italian adventurer in the service of France, to the Cape Fear region. His extremely favorable report to his sponsor probably would have brought French settlers if political conditions in France been different. However, the French king was too involved with internal problems to do anything about Verrazano's report.

Two years later a large gold-seeking Spanish expedition led by Lucas Vasquez de Ayllon of the island of Santo Domingo (now Haiti and the Dominican Republic) came to the Cape Fear. Although he and his settlers did not remain, they did stay long enough to build a ship to replace one they had lost on the dreaded Cape of Feare or possibly Frying Pan Shoals. Thus it is thought that the first boat built by Europeans in the New World was built along the shore of Southport or on Bald Head Island. To de Ayllon the river was known as the Rio Jordan. Bald Head Island or the Cape of Feare was known as Cape Romano. The area surrounding the river and the island was called "The Land of Ayllon."

While the Spanish did not give up their claim to any part of the New World, they failed to occupy much of it because they were continually moving in their search for gold. For the most part they had expelled the French, but now they had to contend with the rising nation of England. When Henry VII came to the throne he and his Tudor successors led England toward importance in world trade. English farmers, finding it difficult to make a living on their small farms, crowded into the cities creating extreme social problems. The wealthy and influential middle class merchants who had found wealth in world trade, organized stock companies to further their holdings. From these two factors came a renewed interest in settling the New World. Nationalism reached an unusually high level during the reign of Queen Elizabeth I. From this atmosphere a breed of men known as the English seadogs sailed forth to seek wealth and fame in America. Sometimes the adventurers were sponsored by trade companies and at other times by the Crown.

Sir Humphrey Gilbert made the first attempt to further England's claim by actual occupation of the land. Queen Elizabeth gave him letters patent to achieve his goal, but he died in 1583 while attempting to establish a colony for England in Newfoundland.

At his death, the patent rights passed to his half-brother, the gallant Sir Walter Raleigh. Sir Walter was interested in finding a more southerly climate than found by his brother. In 1584 he sent

14

out two seafaring men, Philip Amadas and Arthur Barlowe, to find a site for a colony in a favorable climate. Amadas and Barlowe sailed along the North Carolina coast and took back to England a glowing report of praise for the region they called Virginia in honor of the Virgin Queen. Because of the favorable report, Sir Walter Raleigh sent out a group of colonists in 1585 under the leadership of Ralph Lane. The colony, landing on what came to be known as Roanoke Island, was an ill-fated venture. By summer of the following year the men were facing starvation. When Sir Francis Drake, a fellow Englishman on his way back home from St. Augustine, stopped at Roanoke to check on the colony, he saw their terrible plight and invited them to return to England with him. The settlement which has been called "Roanoke Hundred" came to an abrupt end.

Still determined to establish a colony in America, Sir Walter did not give up after the failed Roanoke venture. In 1587 he sent out another group, including women and children, to Roanoke. This new group was led by Captain John White, whose granddaughter, Virginia Dare, was the first child born of English parents in America. This settlement was soon beset with serious problems and ended in failure. Many interesting and intriguing theories continue to be advanced about the fate of this "Lost Colony," but none have ever been proved.

As England became involved in a long, drawn-out war with Spain, colonizing efforts ceased for a time. However, when peace came in 1604, interest in the settlement of colonies in America was revived. This renewed interest was prompted by the large and politically influential Virginia Company. Chartered in 1606, the company had associates and financiers of Sir Walter Raleigh among its stockholders. The Virginia Company established the first permanent colony in America in 1607 at Jamestown, Virginia. Several decades later the first permanent settlers in North Carolina came from this growing Virginia settlement.

Within the next few years the English empire expanded rapidly. Its many colonies covered a wide area of the New World including Bermuda and Barbados. In 1629 King Charles I granted to his Attorney General, Sir Robert Heath, a charter for the American territory which lay between 31 and 36 degrees north latitude, the territory to reach from the Atlantic to the Pacific. This region, incorporated under the name of Carolana in honor of King Charles, included the Cape Fear area. Heath failed to settle his grant and soon assigned it to George, Lord Berkeley. In less than two months, Lord Berkeley assigned part of the grant to four others. They also failed to colonize the area and the grant remained only on paper.

Soon after the granting of the Heath Charter, a strong political controversy developed between the Crown and Parliament which culminated in England's Civil War of the 1640s. Charles I was beheaded and his son and heir, Charles Stuart, fled to the Continent. In 1649 peace returned to England and for eleven years the country was governed as a commonwealth under Oliver Cromwell. Upon Cromwell's death, Charles Stuart returned from Europe in 1660 to become Charles II. The time following the Restoration was a dynamic one for England and her colonies and had a profound effect on the Cape Fear region.

Due to harsh winters, some Puritan settlers in the Massachusetts Bay Colony were interested in moving to a milder climate. They had heard about the Cape Fear region and sent Captain William Hilton of their colony to explore the area. Hilton, aboard his ship *Adventure*, sailed "from Charles Towne in New Engld ye 14 Aug. 1662." On October 4, 1662, he sailed into the river which he called Charles River, now known as the Cape Fear. As he sailed up the river, he and the crew visited and made friends with the Indians while studying the land for its suitability for farming and cattle raising. He found the situation so encouraging that he "did purchase and buy ye sd. river and ye lands about it, of ye Natives," who called the river "Sapona."

Hilton's report to the Puritan settlers urged them "not to delay to possess it." The group was so impressed with the report that they immediately asked their agent in England to negotiate with the Crown for a charter to confirm Hilton's purchase from the Indians. The New Englanders, however, did not wait to receive the answer from the king and traveled to the Lower Cape Fear in the late winter of 1663. On April 4, not yet knowing what was happening on the political front in the Mother Country, they arranged a return to New England. Before their agent could make any negotiations with the Crown, King Charles II had issued a charter on March 24, 1663 for the old Heath Grant. This charter, made to eight of his friends known as the Lords Proprietors, was an expression of gratitude for their help in restoring his crown.

No one knows why the New England settlers stayed in the Cape Fear region only a few weeks and left angrily. Perhaps it was an unusually cold winter which reminded them of the ones in New England, or perhaps they did not find all of the favorable conditions that Hilton had promised. Another probability is that Sir William Berkeley, the Governor of Virginia and a Lords Proprietor, learned of the arrival of the New Englanders and wrote back to England: "Two hundred families of New England, wee hear are seated a little to the south of us." Since they were in the area without permission from the Crown or the Lords Proprietors, Berkeley probably sent a message that they were not welcome. The religious differences between the Puritans and the Church of England were also likely considerations. One of the settlers reported later that:

> Came a yong man very hastily & prevailed with one of the 2 agents of mr. Paines to goe on board mr. Longs ship from when in a little time aftr Long returned Ashore . . . saying wee have nothing to doe but to goe home.

The settlers were highly upset and made arrangements to leave immediately. Because of their haste to leave, their cattle remained behind on an island in the river which is thought by some to be Bald Head. Also, in their anger, they left a message on an island post addressed to any who might come to settle. The message was most uncomplimentary to the land and the river containing words of discouragement for readers. This message did establish a rather bad reputation for the area as another failed colonization attempt.

William Hilton, by now living on the island of Barbados, was still convinced there was great potential for a settlement on the Cape Fear River. Even though word of the New Englanders' unfavorable remarks on the region had already reached the Barbadians, Captain Hilton was able to persuade a large number of them that the Cape Fear region was suitable for settlement. The Barbadians organized an exploration expedition of the Carolina coast. With Hilton as commander, the expedition sailed from Barbados on August 10, 1663. On October 16 the expedition arrived at the river once called the Charles River by Hilton. Again reporting favorable conditions, he referred to the river as "Cape Fair River." Back in Barbados, however, disagreements had arisen among the backers of the project, and it was abandoned.

John Vassall of Barbados was one of those who had contributed financing for Hilton's second voyage to Carolina. He was determined that a colony should be established there and arranged to transport a group from Barbados to the Cape Fear for settlement. Vassall and his followers landed on May 29, 1664, thus beginning the first lasting European settlement in the Lower Cape Fear region. In November the settlement was incorporated into a county called Clarendon, one of the three established by the Proprietors in the Carolinas. The recently knighted Sir John Yeamans of Barbados was named Governor of Clarendon County by the Lords Proprietors. John Vassall was appointed to serve as Deputy-Governor and Attorney-General. A trading center known as Charles Towne was established about twenty miles upriver. Several smaller settlements were started at other sites along the west bank of the river.

The settlers encountered many hardships including serious problems with the Indians because the settlers mistreated them. Also, the system of allotting the land, as set up by the Proprietors, was unfair and totally unacceptable. Governor Yeamans did not even visit Clarendon County until the fall of 1665, when he passed through while heading further south to Port Royal which was his personal choice for a settlement. Because of the neglect of the Governor and the Lords Proprietors, the hardships endured, and the unpopular system of land allotment, the settlers began moving to other colonies. By the autumn of 1667 the Proprietors closed the land office and the county was completely abandoned. Once more the Indians of the Lower Cape Fear region had the land to themselves.

From the beginning of the Lords Proprietors ownership of the lands in their charter there had been much dissatisfaction as to the division of Carolina. Those living in the Albemarle region especially felt neglected in favor of the southern part known at that time as Craven County. The controversy became so heated that on December 7, 1710, the Lords Proprietors, hoping to provide a more stable and efficient government, decided to separate the grant into North and South Carolina. They then appointed Edward Hyde as Governor of North Carolina "independent of the Governor of South Carolina."

Meanwhile, piracy was gaining a foothold along the North Carolina coast as the many inlets and coves made good hiding places for pirate ships. Other troubles along the coast increased as well, especially with the Indians. In 1715 there was an Indian uprising with troops from both North and South Carolina joining forces to put down the uprising and also subdue the pirate menace. Colonel Maurice Moore of South Carolina, then living in the Albemarle region of North Carolina, led his troops through the Lower Cape Fear region to fight the Indians. After several bloody battles, the power of the Cape Fear Indians was ended.

In the late summer of 1718, Stede Bonnet, known as the *Gentleman Pirate*, entered the Cape Fear River with his ship the *Royal James* and two other captured vessels. The *Royal James* needed repairs and the pirates wanted to divide their booty while the repairs were being made. On September 26th Colonel William Rhett of Charleston, still seeking to rid the Carolinas of the pirate threat and hearing of Bonnet's presence, came with his expedition into the harbor to capture the pirates. After a vicious battle of many hours, Colonel Rhett returned to Charleston with his prisoners. Upon the execution of Stede Bonnet in Charleston on December 10, 1718, piracy on the Cape Fear was ended. Today Bonnet's Creek which crosses Moore Street below the old Smithville Burying Grounds, and Rhett Street are the only reminders of Southport's *Age of Piracy*.

In 1723 George Burrington became Governor of North Carolina. Finally North Carolina had a leader who was interested in the Cape Fear area and understood how important the deep water harbor, where the Cape Fear and Elizabeth Rivers entered the ocean, could be in the settlement of the state. Burrington explored the area for himself, encouraged the development of the Cape Fear section, and took up a patent for 5,000 acres in his name.

A boundary dispute arose between the two Carolinas. At one time South Carolina claimed that its boundary came to the west bank of the Cape Fear. At another time the boundary was claimed to be somewhere in the vicinity of what is now Shallotte. In this time of disputes and general unrest, several families from the Charleston and Goose Creek areas of South Carolina came to the Lower Cape Fear seeking large land grants. Maurice Moore, familiar with the land where he fought the Indian wars, had sparked the interest of many who came. Among the others who came were Roger Moore (brother of Maurice), Alexander Lillington, Samuel Swann, Edward Mosely, and Charles Harrison. The earliest grant is dated June 3, 1725. All grants were for immense tracts of land and the grantees were all related either by blood or marriage, causing them to become widely known as "the Family." As a group "the Family" exerted a tremendous political influence.

Brunswick, the first town in the Lower Cape Fear area, was laid out by Maurice Moore in 1726 and was named to honor George I of England, a member of the German House of Brunswick. Lots were sold to the increasing number of settlers arriving to live in the town.

England was having troubles with Spain and France, and it was felt that the entrance to the Cape Fear River was a most vulnerable spot with the new town in danger from enemies entering the harbor. In April 1745, during the administration of Governor Gabriel Johnston, a legislative act was passed giving the governor authority to appoint a council on the defense of the Cape Fear. In July 1745, a site on the bluff overlooking the Cape Fear River was finally decided upon and work began on what was referred to as "Johnston's Fort." Construction progress was slow on the fort which was to be the primary defense of the Cape Fear River, the port of Brunswick, and a new town called Wilmington. The fort was still unfinished when two Spanish ships entered the harbor on September 3, 1748, with the intention of capturing the slaves building the fort. As it was Sunday the slaves were not working but were at Brunswick which was raided by the Spanish. They were finally driven off by armed men from Brunswick and the surrounding area. During the skirmish, one of the Spanish ships was sunk.

The Spanish raid intensified efforts to complete the fort which was declared finished in April 1749. Johnston's Fort was small and poorly constructed. Manned by only one officer and two men, there were four rusty cannons to guard the fort. In an attempt to control commerce on the river, the fort was named a quarantine station in 1751.

During the administration of Governor Arthur Dobbs, appointed Governor in 1754 following the death of Gabriel Johnston, the fort was in such deplorable condition that Dobbs became concerned. He successfully pleaded with the authorities in England for more arms and ammunition. Some help was forthcoming, and Captain John Dalrymple was appointed as the first commander of the fort.

Construction troubles were not over. An Inspection Committee in 1759 reported that the fort was in very poor condition and needed repairs. William Dry of Brunswick was awarded a contract for repairs. He used a material called tapia, a mixture of lime, oyster shells, and sand which was supposed to harden into a very strong substance. Instead, the poorly mixed tapia crumbled into small pieces when the guns were fired.

When Governor Dobbs received the message of the death of

George II in 1760, he called the Provincial Council together and had the accession of George III proclaimed at Brunswick. He also had the "militia drawn out and a triple discharge from Fort Johnston of 21 guns and from all the ships in the River."

In 1761 a hurricane opened New Inlet several miles up the river which allowed vessels to enter the Cape Fear area without coming within cannon range of Fort Johnston. This further diminished the importance of the fort which still housed a small garrison never more than a hundred men until the outbreak of the American Revolution.

Seeking to gain more revenue from the colonies, England passed the Stamp Act triggering a storm of protest. In 1766 when the HMS *Diligence* sailed up the river with a cargo of the hated stamps, there was an uprising in the town of Brunswick and the cargo was not unloaded.

Protests and uprisings continued in various sections of the state as events moved closer to open rebellion by the American colonies and a break with England. Robert Howe, representing Brunswick County in the General Assembly, was favored by Governor William Tryon to replace John Dalrymple as commander of Fort Johnston. Upon Dalrymple's death, Tryon appointed Howe to succeed Dalrymple. After Howe had served only a year, Captain John Collet appeared with a ministry commission as commander of the Fort. When Collet left the state in 1769, Tryon reinstated Howe to the post. Captain Howe was able to repair and improve the fort and increased the troops garrisoned there to twenty-five by 1773.

Tryon left North Carolina for New York in 1771 and was replaced by Josiah Martin. Immediately upon coming to the state Martin became involved in a political situation with Robert Howe whom he intensely disliked. Shortly afterward the governor found a means of replacing Howe and renamed John Collet commander of the fort.

As the American rebellion intensified, Royal Governor Martin fled from the Governor's Palace in New Bern and came to Fort Johnston and his friend Collet for protection, arriving at the fort on June 2, 1775. His further incentive for the move was that the British man-of-war *Cruizer* was anchored offshore. While Martin was in residence at Fort Johnston it became the seat of Loyalist government for North Carolina. Alan McDonald, husband of the famous Flora McDonald and a leading Loyalist in the colony, came in disguise to confer with the governor.

Martin was not known for his good disposition or tactfulness and soon made known his dissatisfaction with things at the fort. He wrote that the fort was "a most contemptible thing, fit neither for place of arms nor an asylum for the friends of the government . . ." Further, he became dissatisfied with Captain Collet.

Because of increasing patriot activity in the Cape Fear area and a general protest over his visit from McDonald, Governor Martin did not remain at the fort very long. Still seeking a refuge, he moved his offices offshore to the warship *Cruizer*, still anchored in the harbor. From there, he ordered Collet to spike the fort's guns. Collet spiked the guns and collected the small arms and ammunition and took them aboard the *Cruizer*. Returning to Fort Johnston, Collet pushed the spiked cannon over the walls of the fort. Led by Robert Howe, patriot forces from Brunswick and the surrounding area burned the fort, its buildings, and the nearby buildings belonging to Captain Collet on July 19, 1775.

Later General Cornwallis placed some of his men at the site and on Bald Head Island but there was no more real activity at Fort Johnston during the American Revolution. It was against this background that the Town of Smithville, the name by which our town was first known, came into being.

A Town Is Born
1792-1860

The year was 1792. The American Revolution had been fought and won. President George Washington had received a majority of the electoral votes in the second national election and had reluctantly agreed to serve a second term. The new Federal City was under construction. It was just five years since the ''miracle'' at Philadelphia had occurred, binding thirteen colonies as the United States of America through a form of government never yet tried. There was a feeling of excitement and exuberance throughout the land as the American people began the building of their new nation.

North Carolina ratified the Constitution and had been admitted to the Union. The new capital city of Raleigh had been laid out, and Richard Dobbs Spaight, a great-nephew of Colonial Governor Arthur Dobbs, was serving as North Carolina's governor. A move was under way to encourage people to settle in North Carolina, and several petitions had already been submitted to the General Assembly asking for grants of large tracts of land on which to build towns.

The Brunswick County seat of government had been moved to the plantation of John Bell in a little community on the banks of the Lockwood Folly River. Brunswick's population stood at 3,071, almost evenly balanced between blacks and whites, as shown by the first Federal Census taken in 1790. The county was entirely rural with vast areas of undeveloped land yet to be claimed. Roads were almost nonexistent and the people depended on the rivers and streams, not only for much of their food, but for moving from place to place in the county.

In the town of Wilmington, a thriving port almost sixty years old, lived a young man named Joshua Potts who was very much interested in starting a town around Fort Johnston which overlooked the mouth of the Cape Fear River. Years later, as an old man,

Mr. Potts would write about the events that led to his interest in establishing a town around the fort.

At the time of the American Revolution, Joshua Potts was living at his home in Halifax County. Early in the war he became a wagoner or commissary officer supplying goods and materials for the North Carolina troops, particularly around Hillsborough. Many references to him and his work can be found in the *Colonial and State Records of North Carolina*. After the Revolution, he moved to Wilmington where he became a merchant, lawyer, surveyor, and broker. He became involved in the town government as well as his business and professional activities.

In 1786 Joshua became ill with a "debilitating fever". After he "received medical attendance", as he put it, he improved somewhat but was still weak and had no appetite. His good friend, Captain John Brown, was master of a packet that plied between Wilmington and Charleston, making regular stopovers at Fort Johnston. Captain Brown had become very friendly with the Fort Johnston men and decided to ask Joshua Potts to accompany him on a trip down the river to the fort. He felt that the sea air would be beneficial to Potts. Joshua agreed, and the two set out in an open boat for the trip downstream. At noon the Captain served a "cold collation" and Joshua was able to eat a small amount. Upon reaching Fort Johnston, Joshua was feeling much better, and his appetite had returned. The men camped out for a day or so and enjoyed the company of the men at Fort Johnston and the area river pilots. The pilots had built their small homes near the water's edge in order to move quickly when a ship was to be guided over the dangerous Frying Pan Shoals, through the channel, and upriver to the port of Wilmington. There was much rivalry among the pilots because only twelve could serve at one time. They paid an annual license fee and were under the control of the commander of Fort Johnston for their orders.

After his little vacation trip, Joshua returned to Wilmington fully recovered from his fever and gave all the credit to the "salubrious breezes" he had enjoyed at Fort Johnston. He felt strongly that the area would be a delightful place for a town and lost no time in discussing his idea with his fellow Wilmingtonians, especially his friends John Huske and Captain Brown. Huske served on the Wilmington town council and had been a delegate to the North Carolina convention that ratified the U. S. Constitution. He was interested in Potts' idea and encouraged him to make plans to carry out the suggestion. Thus began Joshua Potts' persistent dream of a town to be located at the mouth of the Cape Fear River.

Several years later, after Joshua married, he returned to the fort with his young family for another vacation. This time, instead of camping out, he rented the loft of a house from Joseph Swain, one of the river pilots. Mrs. Potts had to cook their meals over a camp fire and, on one occasion, the wild hogs got close enough to run off with the hot cakes she was making. However, such events seemed just a minor inconvenience to Joshua who stated that while they were at the fort they "breathed in health and rough pleasure". Undoubtedly Mrs. Potts agreed that it was rough, though she may not have thought it such a pleasure. How she must have longed that summer for her Wilmington kitchen and the fenced-in yard where her children could play in safety. Mr. Potts, though, continued to be enamored with the fort area and wanted others to enjoy it as he did.

In a letter to Potts from John Huske dated October 18, 1790, Mr. Huske suggested that Joshua not wait any longer to devise a plan to have a town laid out around the fort. He further suggested that his friend draw up a petition to the General Assembly and obtain the proper number of signatures for presentation at the next session. Potts, pleased that his friend felt as he did, went ahead with the petition. He was further encouraged by Mr. Charles Gause who lived in the Town Creek area. The petition was prepared, and the signatures obtained. When it was presented to Benjamin Smith, a wealthy plantation owner then representing Brunswick County in the General Assembly, he refused to introduce the bill. It is believed that his reluctance was due to his close friendship with some of the river pilots who, of course, might stand to lose the lands they had laid claim to around the fort.

Joshua Potts and Captain John Brown were disappointed, but they did not let the dream die. They continued to talk up the idea, and the following summer and fall they returned to live at the fort during the good weather. In order to have more acceptable dwellings for their families, the two men had prefabricated houses built in Wilmington and floated them down the river on lighters or barges. The buildings were then erected along the beach.

About twelve months after the first petition had been turned down by Benjamin Smith, Charles Gause, who was still very much interested in the building of a new town, approached Joshua Potts with another plan. Gause stated that if Potts would draw up a second petition that he would get it signed and see that Benjamin Smith would introduce and support it in the General Assembly. Joshua quickly agreed. True to his word, Mr. Gause, who was evidently a man of considerable influence, took the petition, obtained the signatures, and then visited Mr. Smith. In no uncertain terms, Mr. Gause made it very plain to Smith that if he did not introduce the necessary bill and get it passed, he would never represent Brunswick County in the Legislature again. Smith then introduced the bill in the General Assembly meeting in New Bern. On November 15, 1792, the bill was passed and the charter was issued under the date of December 31, 1792. (Appendix A).

The river pilots were among those who signed the petition presented to the General Assembly. The petition emphasized that "the erection of a town on the west side of the Cape Fear River will be attended with a variety of beneficial effects to the health, commerce and convenience of said county and those adjoining . . ."

As provided in the charter, the new town was named Smithville. Some say that the name was chosen by some of Benjamin Smith's rival politicians because they thought the tiny town would fail and thus reflect adversely on Smith. Others believe the name was given to honor Smith as the person who introduced the bill in the legislature, saw it through to enactment, and became an ardent supporter of the town which bore his name.

Joshua Potts, Charles Gause, William Espey Lord, Robert Howe, Jr. and Benjamin Smith, named in the charter as the town's first commissioners, lost no time holding a meeting to make plans for setting up Smithville. Their first meeting was held in Wilmington on January 26, 1793, at "the house of Amaziah Jocelin." Joshua Potts and Benjamin Smith drew the map showing the hundred lots that were to comprise the town, together with the waterskirts and land for the common use.

In further compliance with instructions given in the charter, advertisements appeared in the Fayetteville and Wilmington newspapers announcing the second Saturday of March 1793 as the date of the sale of the lots and stating the terms of purchase. No one could purchase more than six lots in his or her name and the purchase price was to be forty shillings per lot, or approximately four dollars.

Most of the lots at the sale were purchased for by residents of Wil-

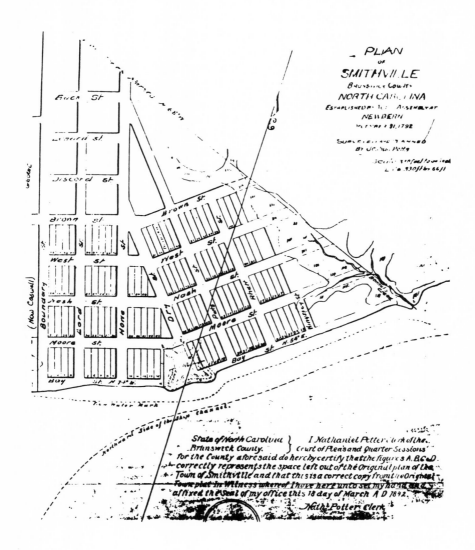

The original town map in 1792 included 100 lots. Beginning at the corner of Caswell and Bay Streets they were numbered from west to east, running northward to the intersection of Rhett and Brown Streets. The unusual outline in the lower portion of the map is the Fort Johnston reservation, which from the outset has been the focal point of the community.

mington, either to build homes or as real estate investments. Joshua Potts bought several in his name and in the names of his wife and others. Benjamin Smith also bought a number of lots with some of them being in the name of his wife's parents, William and Mary Ann Dry. The other three commissioners purchased lots too.

Joshua Potts became the first clerk for the town. He made his first entries in a book made of "throw away" paper to be transferred to a permanent book called the Town of Smithville Record Book. Part of his book made from scrap paper is in the archives of the Lower Cape Fear Historical Society and is referred to as a "waste book." So far as is known, none of the permanent book has ever been found. Very little is known of the town's earliest years, but a few items have been gleaned from newspapers of the day, census records, and land records. In 1800 when the second Federal Census was taken, Smithville was eight years old. The county population was then 4,110, but we do not know how many of those lived in Smithville. Homes had been built in the town, but some residents came to live in those homes only during the summer months. However, there were enough permanent residents that Smithville, then a part of the Bladen Circuit of the Methodist Conference, was visited by circuit riders who held meetings in tents. A large number of the Wilmingtonians who had built homes in Smithville were communicants of St. James Church in Wilmington.

In June 1798 Philip Williams came to Smithville opening a school that was to teach arithmetic, navigation, surveying, algebra, and geometry. His advertisement in a Wilmington newspaper stated that boarding facilities were available. In October, the Town Commissioners decided to erect a frame building 24 by 16 feet for a temporary school house. It was specified that the building should be built a few inches above the ground on brick pillars, with weatherboarding, shingles, flooring, and a brick chimney. This so fits the description of an old building given to the Southport Historical Society by Pfizer Corporation that one can only wonder if it might be the temporary schoolhouse as planned by the Commissioners.

In March of the following year, a group known as Trustees of the Smithville Academy, one of whom was Benjamin Smith, met to make plans to hold a lottery for the purpose of raising money to erect an academy in Smithville. There was definitely a deep interest among the founders to provide education to the youth.

As an indication of the town's population in 1800, there were more than fifty citizens, including thirty-six children, who took part in a elaborate memorial service on February 13th to honor George Washington who had died the previous December. The "troops at Fort Johnston" were also involved. On the Fourth of July of the following year there was a stirring and loud celebration at Fort Johnston beginning at sunrise with a 16-gun salute. At noon, Captain John Brown of the revenue cutter *Diligence* fired another salute. In mid-afternoon, officers and citizens gathered in the garden of a Mr. Gamache to offer toasts — with each toast followed by the discharge of a cannon.

An even bigger celebration was held in 1804. The day began with a discharge of artillery at Fort Johnston where Lt. John Fergus was in command. At noon, the *Diligence*, still under the command of Captain John Brown, gave a salute, and the citizens assembled on the waterfront responded with cheers. A Mrs. McDonald then gave a roast beef dinner presided over by Captain Brown and Lt. Fergus. After dinner there were toasts, more firing of cannons, and the singing of "appropriate" songs. One of the toasts was to the town: "To the Town of Smithville - May the exertions of the founder meet with the reward due his merits." The festivities were finished off with a grand ball in the evening. Smithville citizens have always loved a celebration - especially on the Fourth of July!

In the fall of 1804, Benjamin Smith and Lt. Joseph Gardner Swift of the Army Engineers were ordered by the U. S. War Department to begin the rebuilding of Fort Johnston. Smith's slaves began the burning of oyster shells for lime to be used in the construction. Lt. Swift had already uncovered some of the original parts of the old fort and the new battery was begun. In 1805 a hospital was constructed at the fort to serve the garrisoned soldiers and any sailors entering or leaving the harbor. The hospital structure was moved from the northeast side of the Fort Johnston reservation in 1889 and converted to residential use. A report dated December 6, 1870, from the Surgeon General's Office of the War Department in Washington, gives a description of the hospital at Fort Johnston that fits the description and measurements of a building that was moved to Bay Street by A. J. (Jack) Robbins for Capt. Tom Morse, a river pilot.

While working together on the rebuilding of Fort Johnston, Benjamin Smith and Lt. Swift developed a strong and lasting friendship. When Lt. Swift married the daughter of John Walker, a resident of Smithville and Wilmington, in June of 1805, Mrs. Smith

Officers Quarters at Fort Johnston, as rebuilt in 1804.

gave a reception for them at the Smith mansion at the corner of Bay and Potts Streets. It was during the reception for the newlyweds that Captain Maurice Moore sent a challenge to his cousin General Benjamin Smith for a duel to settle a family quarrel. Later in the month the duel was fought and Smith was attended by his friend, Joseph Gardner Swift. General Smith was seriously wounded and was brought back from the Boundary House (on the North Carolina/South Carolina border) to Smithville where he was treated by the two surgeons at the fort. Mrs. Smith came to Smithville from their plantation at Belvedere to be with her husband and shortly thereafter had the general moved to their Wilmington residence where he recuperated. Years later, after the death of the then impoverished General Smith, Joseph Gardner Swift returned to Smithville for a visit. When he learned that there had been no stone erected at the grave of Mrs. Smith, Swift had a marble slab placed over her grave at Brunswick Town inscribed: "In memory of the Excellent Lady, Sarah Rhett Dry Smith, who died the 21st of November 1821, aged 59 years."

By 1806 the town had grown to the extent that the General Assembly was requested to enact a bill providing:

The lands belonging to the State adjoining the Town of Smithville shall be sold under the direction of three commissioners, to-wit John Conniers (Conyers), Benjamin Blaney and Samuel Potter, who shall give bond and security for their faithful performance as such . . . and said Commissioners shall cause an accurate survey of the said lands to be made and that it be laid off in such convenient lotts or percells as will enhance the value thereof . . . shall execute good and sufficient title for the respective lotts and percells.

Two years later another bill was passed by the General Assembly that was to make some decided changes to life in the little town. This bill approved the removal of the county seat of Brunswick County from Lockwood Folly to Smithville as soon as a courthouse, jail, and stocks could be built. Naturally, this sparked a lot of controversy from people living in other areas of the county. The opposition to the move was so great that people living in the western part petitioned the legislature to set up another county made up of parts of Brunswick and Bladen Counties. The new county was named for Christopher Columbus.

Brunswick County Courthouse, Smithville, about 1808.

The new Brunswick County buildings were to be erected by private funds and many citizens of Smithville subscribed to their cost. They were quite proud of the courthouse, a one-story brick building. By 1826 more space was needed, so a larger courthouse

31

was built. The original building was then sold and removed from the lot. Progress was slow, but eventually the new building was ready for use. As the county's business grew in the early 1850s, so did the need for a still larger courthouse. Once again the courthouse was torn down and a new one took its place. This time a two-story brick building was erected by architect-builder W. D. Morrell.

Soon another event took place that was to have an effect on life in Smithville. In August 1807 Robert Fulton had perfected his steam engine and had successfully made a trip with his steamboat on the Hudson River between New York and Albany. Before long small steamers were also plying the Cape Fear.

At this time another conflict between England and the United States was brewing. Federal and State authorities felt that the mouth of the Cape Fear River would be vulnerable in the event of any open hostilities. As a result, the brick barracks and guard house at Fort Johnston were completed. Troops were moved in and supplies that had been stored in Wilmington for ten years were moved to the blockhouse in 1810. The State Legislature asked Congress for an appropriation to strengthen the defenses even further, but it was not granted.

On July 1, 1811, Smithville's first post office was opened with John Conyers as the first postmaster. However, his health failed, and he died within a few months. On October 1st he was succeeded by Benjamin Blaney.

In May 1812, war with the British seemed to be a certainty. The U.S. Secretary of War asked Governor William Hawkins of North Carolina to have the 7,000 man North Carolina Detached Militia ready to march, with their own guns, to any place necessary to defend the coast. Major General Thomas Pinckney of Charleston was to assign the troops.

On June 18, 1812, the United States declared war on Great Britain. Immediately after the declaration of war, General Pinckney requested four companies of either infantry or artillery to report to Fort Johnston to garrison it against possible attack. These troops arrived without uniforms and had to buy them on credit. At first there were not even any arrangements to feed the troops and the townspeople took it upon themselves to feed the soldiers. The troops at the fort, under the command of Colonel John A. Lillington, were quartered in Smithville. Wet weather prevented them from pitching tents at the fort which was not equipped to house all the men. Soon work was started on log houses covered with clapboards to serve as winter quarters for the men. They were encouraged to catch fish in the river to supplement their slim food supply.

To make matters even worse, yellow fever broke out. There seems to be no record of how many of the troops and townspeople were affected, but eleven sailors died while ashore and were buried in the Old Smithville Cemetery. The little four-year-old son of the fort's doctor was also stricken and died.

Fort Johnston had artillery, but there were no men stationed there who knew how to fire the guns. The citizens of Wilmington, as well as Smithville, felt defenseless and were very concerned. The British kept tightening their blockade. In spite of this, the citizens of Smithville continued about their daily affairs as best they could.

The British had not appeared in the river by September of 1812, and General Pinckney decided the militia could return to their homes. These men went home without being paid although they had been promised pay ranging from $8.00 to $12.00 a month, plus $124.00 for enlisting and a bounty of 160 acres of land when the war was over. The advertisement encouraging them to join had stated that it was "A Golden Opportunity." The militia was to be replaced by a smaller contingent of "regulars."

Patriotism was still running high in Smithville and the 1813 Fourth of July celebration was a loud one with a salute of 13 guns from Fort Johnston. The citizens gathered at the courthouse where Lt. Rouse read the *Declaration of Independence* and George Washington's *Farewell Address*. A prayer was offered, and at noon 18 guns were fired from the revenue cutter *Diligence*. At 1 p.m. a salute of 18 guns came from Fort Johnston. At 2 p.m. a dinner was held at the hotel of Samuel Potter with Joshua Potts presiding. Toasts were offered with each accompanied by a song. At 9 p.m. there was a display of fireworks designed by Lt. Rouse.

There was still some apprehension that more protection was needed along the coast. The British had continued sneak attacks at points along the coast and once sent two ships and a brig which remained at the main bar for two or three days, but eventually sailed away taking no action. Three river pilots were captured by the British, but it is unknown who they were or what happened to them. Joshua Potts submitted to Governor Hawkins a lengthy report about the fortifications on the coast with his recommendations as to Fort Johnston. Potts also urged the construction of a fort on Oak Island, but no action was taken on his report.

The war ended in December 1814 with the signing of a peace treaty, but it was not until February 11, 1815, that the news reached New York. Within a few days all recruiting ceased; the militia and enlisted men at Fort Johnston were sent home.

Robert Howe, Jr. and Dennis Hankins advertised for bids to construct a Methodist Church to measure 30 by 50 feet. The General Assembly passed a bill declaring "certain waterskirts fronting the Town of Smithville permanent property". Heretofore, these waterskirt lots had been leased out for wharves and warehouses. The act passed by the General Assembly does not mention it, but we know from newspaper accounts and other sources that there were taverns, stores, and boarding houses on these lots.

A short time later Joshua Potts reported to Federal authorities that erosion was causing the destruction of the lighthouse on Bald Head Island built in 1794. In this report he also stated that the extreme shallowness of the water on the main bar, along with the lighthouse problem was making navigation very difficult. The next April Congress appropriated $16,000 for the erection of a new lighthouse. Contractor Daniel S. Way was to complete the project in 1818. Until then mariners used General Smith's "large white house in Smithville" as their point of reference.

In 1817 the steamer *Prometheus* was constructed in Beaufort by Captain Otway Burns. The next year it was purchased by a stock company based in Wilmington to operate as the first steamboat on the Cape Fear. The first run was made on June 20, 1818, and the scheduled time from Wilmington to Smithville was four hours, depending, of course, on the wind and weather. The fare was one dollar each way. When President Monroe visited Wilmington in April 1819, one of the special events for him was an excursion on the *Prometheus* from Wilmington to Smithville. By 1896 the scheduled time had been cut to two hours, including stops at all the river landings.

Smithville's population was growing. By 1820 the permanent population was about 300 with an additional two or three hundred part-time residents in the summer and fall to take advantage of the cool breezes and relaxed way of life. With the population growth came the need for a new jail. The Committee for Public Buildings, John C. Baker, John Brown, Jr., and Robert Potter, called for bids to erect a two-story frame jail building 25 by 30 feet. There was to be a pair of stocks and pillory included. Until this time the county had apparently been using the city's jail located at the edge of Franklin Square facing Nash Street. It is not known if the jail called for in the bid was built or not, but it probably was and on the same site as the old city jail. We are told that in 1849 the jail was destroyed by a fire set by an inmate who escaped from his second story cell. In October 1850 bids for a jail were let again. This time the two-story building's measurements were given as 30 by 22 feet with garret added. As late as 1879 a newspaper account tells of eleven persons being crowded into a "one-room jail" at Smithville. In 1904 the building now referred to as the "Old Jail" was constructed for Brunswick County by A. J. Robbins. Located at the corner of Nash and Rhett Streets, the jail was built on land purchased by the county from Miss Kate Stuart. This building housed prisoners until 1971 when it was replaced by the one-story brick building just to the rear of the "Old Jail" facing Rhett Street. The county used the "Old Jail" building as offices for the Sheriff's Department until the county seat was moved to Bolivia in 1978.

Jail and Pillory at Smithville, NC. From Frank Leslie's Newspaper, March 4, 1865. Courtesy of New Hanover County Library.

Congress finally appropriated money for the construction of a fort on Oak Island as requested by Joshua Potts years before. In 1825 work started on the fortification at the tip of Oak Island. The installation was named Fort Caswell in honor of the first governor of North Carolina after it became an independent state. Construction of Fort Caswell was to have a significant effect on Smithville and later, on Southport.

Work on the fort proceeded slowly with erosion a constant problem. As late as February 1836 advertisements in area newspapers asked for laborers who were promised the sum of 50 cents a day. Also, quarries in both North and South Carolina were called upon to submit bids for furnishing the needed stone. It was not until October 1838 that Fort Caswell was announced almost complete at a cost of $473,402.

Following the end of the War of 1812 only a caretaking force of men, with one or two officers, were stationed at Fort Johnston. However, in early summer of 1842 a company of soldiers from New Orleans under the command of Lt. S. L. Fremont arrived at Johnston. This was a rowdy bunch of men who were insubordinate to their officers and terrorized the citizens of the town with their drunkenness and riotous acts. It is not known what means he used, but in February 1843 Lt. Fremont was court martialed at the fort for his "brutal efforts" to control the rioting soldiers. At the trial the townspeople came to his aid and praised him for quelling the riots. Evidently Lt. Fremont was not severely punished because a short time later he was entering into contracts for provisions for Fort Johnston. Colonel Thomas Childs was commander of the fort and Lt. Fremont was commissary officer.

The Stuart House.

In 1842, a boarding house was opened on the waterskirts between Potts Street and Rhett Street which would eventually put Smithville "on the map." Mrs. Mary Garland Bensell, a widow with five small children, opened the boarding house as a means of supporting her family. A short while later she married Dr. Charles Henry Stuart, a chemist at Fort Johnston. On April 13, 1844, their daughter Kate was born. Kate would become known as "The Heroine of Smithville" and later as "The Grand Old Lady of North Carolina".

In 1843, feeling a need for an Anglican Church in Smithville, Colonel Childs of Fort Johnston and his men were instrumental in having the Chapel of the Cross erected beside the courthouse and across the street from the fort. The church, later named St. Philip's Episcopal Church in honor of St. Philip's Church at Brunswick Town, has had a long and colorful history.

The Chapel of the Cross, 1843, (now St. Philip's Episcopal Church).

In 1844 and 1845, big celebrations were held on Independence Day. The format was usually the same with gun salutes, the reading of the *Declaration of Independence*, and a grand ball in the evening at Ruggles Hotel. On these occasions a procession was added to the usual Fourth of July festivities. The procession included soldiers from the fort and thirteen young ladies dressed in white representing the thirteen original colonies. They formed the procession at the fort and marched to Chapel of the Cross where they listened to orations.

War came again. On May 13, 1846, Congress declared war on Mexico and a company of Brunswick County volunteers formed to fight in the Mexican War. Lt. Fremont was detached from the Army at Fort Johnston and sent on a recruiting mission in Wilmington. The new recruits were sworn in and sent to Fort Johnston for training. Nine companies had been formed by December, but a fever struck the area and each day saw the death of one or more recruits. The following February influenza took its toll, too, and several cases of mumps were reported.

In spite of death and illness, six full companies and two detachments were finally assembled at Forts Johnston and Caswell awaiting transportation. Lt. Fremont chartered schooners to take the men to Mexico, a trip which took fifteen to twenty days. Lt. Fremont was promoted to the rank of captain. In June 1848 a peace treaty was signed with Mexico, and no further troops came to the forts.

By 1850 Brunswick County had a population of approximately 7,500 people. The Smithville population was made up of 686 black people and 778 white people. This was the first census to list occupations. Smithville District showed ship's carpenters, boat builders, mechanics, tavern keepers, wheelwrights, blacksmiths, coopers, turpentine makers, masons, pilots, and farmers as the major occupations.

Interest in education continued, and in September 1851 the town was asking for proposals for the construction of a three-story "Academy, Temperance Hall, and Masonic Lodge" to be located on "Meeting House Square fronting on Nash Street". Years later, in his memoirs, Dr. W.G. Curtis stated that the building was completed about the same time as the new courthouse.

Located across the street from the Academy, the new two-story brick courthouse replaced an earlier wooden structure on the same site and was finally completed in October of 1854. This building has undergone numerous repairs and alterations in its long history. Because of a clause in the original deed from the Town of Smithville to Brunswick County, the former courthouse is today the Southport City Hall. In the deed dated December 20, 1808, the phrase "reserving always to the said town the rights of said lot and buildings providing the courts should hereafter be removed" appeared. Thus, when the county seat was moved to Bolivia in 1978, the lot and building reverted to the city's ownership.

Also in 1854, two Methodist ministers, James H. Brent and E. M. Pepper, were assigned to the Smithville circuit. Evidently, they lived in Smithville because they, together with Jeremiah Murphy, an "educated Irish teacher and layman of St. Philip's Chapel", began a school for children of the community and county. The school was called an academy and was probably located in the recently built academy-lodge hall.

A few years earlier, Captain John Newland Maffitt, commander of the U.S. Navy schooner *Gallatin*, had come to Smithville as a part of the U. S. Coast Survey. The men of the schooner and their families were housed in the barracks on the Garrison and became a vital part of the social activities of the town, especially in summer when the part-time residents arrived from Wilmington. Captain Maffitt, a most congenial and outgoing person, soon was leading the officers and residents in establishing a successful dramatic company. He is credited with making life much more pleasant for the whole town and wrote to friends about picnics, fishing, excursions, kite flying, and sea bathing to be enjoyed. In addition, he also mentioned that the young ladies and gentlemen often strolled in the moonlight on the Garrison grounds. As late as 1857 Maffitt was still at Fort Johnston. Later, during the Civil War, he distinguished himself in his service to the Confederacy as a blockade runner. James Sprunt, chronicler of the Cape Fear, called him "the bravest of the brave."

The late 1850s brought many changes. In 1857 the nation found itself in a terrible economic panic following a period of wild speculating and investment in real estate. The inevitable crash came and within the next few months a religious revival broke out. The residents of Smithville reacted with fervor as church membership and attendance grew. The panic ended by 1859 as the country was moving inexorably toward Civil War. The number of summer visitors grew along with the town's general population. Thomas D. Meares bought and tore down the old, dilapidated, but once magnificent residence of Benjamin Smith on the corner of Bay and Potts Streets. He then built, on the same site, the beautiful structure which today is known as The Brunswick Inn.

The Brunswick Inn.

Getting their news from river travelers and Wilmington news-papers, Smithville citizens were well aware of the bitter North-South controversy that was becoming more explosive every day. For the next three years they could only watch and wait for the turn of events that would bring a mighty upheaval to their riverside village.

Smithville During The Civil War and Reconstruction 1861-1877

Although the conflict known as the War of Northern Aggression, the War Between the States or the Civil War did not actually begin until the spring of 1861, the events leading to it created restlessness and fear in Smithville. Tensions mounted rapidly in the entire South after 1854 when the Republican Party emerged as the entity around which those opposed to slavery could rally. Some southerners felt their whole way of life was threatened. South Carolina seceded from the Union on December 20, 1860, and soon one state after another followed South Carolina's lead. In North Carolina a "wait and see" attitude prevailed.

With Smithville and Wilmington located on the Cape Fear River, and with Forts Johnston and Caswell manned by small contingents of Federal troops, the citizens were increasingly fearful because of their vulnerable position. Two companies of volunteers, the Smithville Guards and the Cape Fear Minute Men, were organized, and on December 31, 1860, the residents of the two towns sent a letter to North Carolina Governor John W. Ellis requesting permission to take over Fort Johnston and Fort Caswell. Governor Ellis denied the request because such action, with North Carolina still in the Union, would have been insurrection. Very soon after their written request was refused, a delegation from the towns traveled to Raleigh to again ask the governor for permission to take the forts. With only a few men garrisoned at each fort, a takeover would have been fairly easy, but again the Governor denied their request.

Less than a month later, on January 10, 1861, the two volunteer companies of Smithville and Wilmington took matters into their own hands and under the leadership of Colonel John J. Hedrick, captured the forts without incident. When Governor Ellis learned

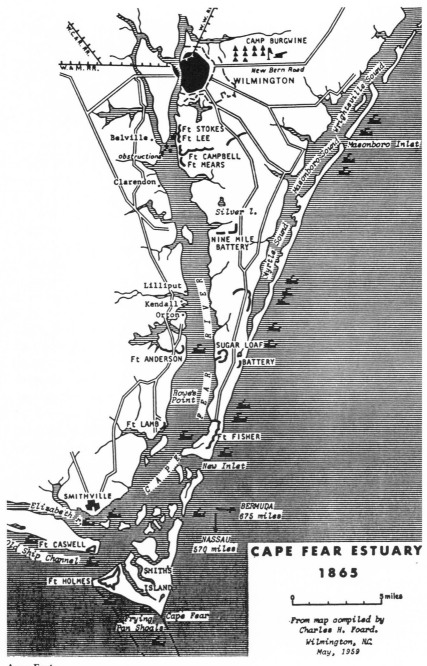

Area Forts.

42

of the action, he ordered the return of the forts to Union troops. Governor Ellis not only was concerned about the return of the forts, he was also disturbed about the conditions at the forts. He wrote to the governor of Georgia saying:

> *The U.S. forts in this area are indefensible. The armament is incomplete and of a very ordinary kind. The best fort, Caswell, has indeed but two serviceable guns and they of light calibre.*

The first violence of the Civil War occurred on January 9, 1861, when a Union supply ship was driven away from Fort Sumter in South Carolina. On April 12, South Carolina troops fired on the Union-held fort and three days later President Lincoln called for troops to end the insurrection. Immediately the Secretary of War wired Governor Ellis for two regiments of militia. Governor Ellis' reply to the Secretary of War said in part "You can get no troops from North Carolina." He then ordered the 13th North Carolina Militia to occupy Fort Johnston, Fort Caswell, and Fort Macon, a fort in Carteret County. Again Fort Johnston and Fort Caswell were taken without incident.

On April 19th, 1861, President Lincoln declared a military and commercial blockade of all southern ports and on the following day the first blockading ship dropped anchor off Smithville. Almost immediately, North Carolina public opinion changed to favor secession. The General Assembly called a convention to vote on the issue and on May 20, 1861, North Carolina left the Union. Within an hour an ordinance was passed ratifying the *Provisional Constitution of the Confederate States of America*. The Confederacy had been formed on February 4, 1861.

The women of Smithville rallied to "the cause." They made a special Confederate flag which was given to the Smithville Guards with great and tearful ceremony. Sophia Ann Drew, the 17-year-old daughter of leading town citizens Mr. and Mrs. Jesse Drew, presented the flag with an enthusiastic speech typical of the fervor felt by the citizenry. (Appendix B)

At the beginning of the war there was much excitement, especially among the young. As the men marched away, bands played stirring music, dainty handkerchiefs were waved, and tears flowed easily as the Smithville women watched loved ones leaving for the battlefields with the flag of "the cause" flying high.

One of the most vital needs for the armies of the Confederacy going to battle was salt. No longer could it be brought in from England or the northern states; now it was imperative that the South manufacture its own. Salt was so important to the war effort that those who produced it were exempt from military service. Several salt works were built in Smithville, and near the inlets along the Elizabeth River, and on Dutchman Creek just west of town. Because investment capital was extremely limited in the town, some of the salt works were financed by Wilmington men.

Captain Thomas M. Thompson, blockade runner.

From the time the first blockading ship anchored off Smithville until the end of the war, Smithville pilots were among those who heroically ran the blockade to bring supplies to the Confederacy. At one time in 1864, thirty-four ships were blockading local waters. The main bar and New Inlet, cut by a hurricane many years before, had to be guarded. Being familiar with the river, the channels, and the maritime conditions, the blockade runners were often able to slip out under cover of darkness. They would then travel to Nassau and other ports bringing back needed materials.

As the blockade tightened, the services of the runners became vital to keeping the Confederacy alive. Smithville's river pilots were men of courage, skill, and daring. With their swift vessels, their intimate knowledge of local waters, and their keen awareness of the dangers of the Frying Pan Shoals, they made many trips through the blockade. Smithville men running the blockade included James Bell, Joseph Bensell, Thomas Brinkman, Julius Dosher, Richard Dosher, C.C. Morse, T.W. Newton, J.W. Potter, William St. George and Thomas M. Thompson.

The Confederate paper money issued was practically worthless and inflation soared. However, the blockade runners were paid in gold with each trip bringing the handsome sum of approximately three thousand dollars for the crew. James Erastus Price, a young boy during the war whose father and uncle were blockade runners, commented years later:

> *Never before nor since has the town of Southport—although over a hundred years old—experienced such prosperity as came to it in the blockade-running days. Danger from capture by the blockaders and the possibility of yellow fever abroad were outweighed, in the minds of numerous pilots of the town, by the golden harvest their services brought . . . The gold so quickly obtained was lavishly spent. Money was plentiful, and, although many communities in the South were suffering for the necessaries of life, the people of the ports of entry were well fed and clothed.*

Captain Thomas Mann Thompson saved much of the gold which he received and after the war built a lovely house which stands today at the corner of Bay and Caswell Streets. Other pilots probably built homes with their hard earned money, but over the years, fires and storms have destroyed many of the fine homes that were once a part of the town.

Captain Thomas M. Thompson's home built about 1868, corner of Bay and Caswell Streets.

After North Carolina seceded from the Union, men entered the Confederate service in ever-increasing numbers. Men from Brunswick County and surrounding counties enlisted at either Fort Johnston or at Fort Caswell where camps of instruction were set up. This brought to the town an air of excitement, but also a feeling of fear and uncertainty. There was no normal life. With mail as their only means of communication, and it very slow, people often gathered at the courthouse, the boarding houses, or around Fort Johnston for news of the war's progress or news about their men in service. Telegraph lines were operating between Smithville and Wilmington, Fort Caswell, and Fort Fisher.

Young James Price, who lived near Fort Johnston, saw much activity there that intrigued him and his pals. They were particularly interested in a Yankee prisoner brought to the fort. Price said that he and the boys did not look upon "the poor lonely fellow, far away from his friends in the North," as an object of pity, but as "a curiosity." The boys listened intently as the blockade runners sat around the waterfront relating their exploits, the dangers they had encountered, and bragging of the vast amount of gold they had earned. The youngsters also were fascinated by the beautiful horses at the fort and the parades held on the parade grounds. Allowed to visit the hospital at Fort Johnston, James Price once watched as a surgeon dressed the wounds of a man hurt in battle. Price said that he was "full of curiosity to see how it was done."

As more Smithville men were called into service, the elderly and children were left to carry on their business of survival. The older men, concerned about so many "strange men" encamped in and around the town, feared for the safety of their women. Several older men called a courthouse meeting and under the leadership of John Bell formed a Home Guard. The next day they began drilling, which proved to be too much for them. As the men marched by their houses, each man simply left the ranks at his home. The Home Guard did not last many hours, but apparently the women and children remained safe.

During the war years the county court met regularly in Smithville, led by the men who were not called into service. From the beginning of the war until its end, the Court of Common Pleas and Quarter Sessions, the county's administrative body, tried to function normally by continuing to levy taxes, appoint road crews, and record legal documents. Due to a smallpox epidemic, the quarterly sessions of March and June 1862 were held at a private home in the county.

In September 1862 yellow fever raged in Wilmington causing many Wilmingtonians to relocate in Smithville to escape the fever. Every house was full. For many it was too late to escape the disease, and they died in Smithville. Only a few Smithville citizens contracted the dreaded disease. The troops stationed at the fort were ordered to leave town and camp in the rural areas until the cooler weather brought an end to the epidemic in October.

The Smithville boarding houses were open during the entire war. Kate Stuart and her mother of the Stuart House, and other town women prepared delicious meals for the men at Fort Johnston. Almost every home had a kitchen garden and chickens, and seafood was easily obtained from the Cape Fear. Surviving letters written by soldiers stationed at the fort indicate families sent in foodstuffs from their farms, pantries, and smokehouses to their kinfolk.

Sidney Lanier, a Southern writer of poetry and prose, at one time was stationed with the Signal Corps at Fort Fisher. He spent time at the Stuart House and became great friends with Miss Kate. He was well liked in the town and wrote to a friend in 1864 saying:

> *With my usual good fortune, I have met here several of the kinds of friends I made two years ago in Wilmington. They are spending the summer here in Smithville, and have introduced me to all the nice people in this truly pleasant village. Insomuch that every day since I have been here various servants, bearing white covered dishes of delicacies, or fruit, or books, with notes of compliments from the ladies might have been seen wending their way toward the Signal Quarters where I reside.*

The war brought fear, heartache, and stress to the town's inhabitants. Yellow fever, small pox, and diphtheria were feared as they swept through the town on several occasions. Also, there was the threat of trouble from the blockaders lying offshore and the Union ships that might enter the harbor.

One night in February 1864, Lt. William B. Cushing, the daring commander of the blockader *Monticello* anchored off shore, made a furtive visit to Smithville. Accompanied by several seamen in a small boat, he rowed silently to the town. There he captured a black man and forced him to lead the way to the quarters of Brigadier General Louis Hebert. As the highest ranking Smithville officer and the commander of heavy artillery of the Cape Fear Department, Hebert was a coveted prize for Cushing. However, General Hebert had gone to Wilmington for the evening. Thwarted in their attempt to capture Hebert, Lt. Cushing and his men took a junior Confederate officer back with them as they quickly left town before anyone knew they had been to Smithville. When this deed was discovered, the villagers felt more unsafe than ever.

Even so, life for the young went on as usual as they played along the riverside with barefeet and rolled up trousers. James Price said that the marshes teemed with marsh hens' nests, sheepshead and trout waited for the boys as they fished at "Nancy's Rock", and the terrapin laid their eggs for them at Caswell Beach where the "wild plums hung in mellow readiness." These same wild plums also grew in profusion on the bluffs overlooking the river in Smithville.

Price mentioned that the Cushing raid did not weigh on his youthful mind very long. He stated that the camp with its white tents, bravely-clad warriors, and glittering weapons claimed his fancy to the exclusion of fears. "Above all," he said, "the dashing cavalry officers, with all the accoutrements of their positions, on dress parade, were to me the perfection of beauty and romance."

The most poignant portion of James Price's memoirs is his description of the battle of Fort Fisher which he watched atop his home near Fort Johnston. From his vantage point he saw smoke rising in great clouds from the guns of the warships, while all the windows in town rattled "as if a storm were beating against them." All day the battle raged while anxiety hung over the town. The citizens knew if Fort Fisher fell the enemy would soon be among them. The mighty guns continued their onslaught from January 13, 1865, until the afternoon of the 15th when a decrease in the sound of firing caused the people of Smithville to hope that the Federals had been defeated. Such was not the case. News came during the night that the Confederacy was in Union hands. Later Rear Admiral David B. Porter, Union Commander of the North Atlantic Squadron, stated that this battle was the most terrible fight he had ever seen.

Shortly after the fall of Fort Fisher, the Confederate troops at Fort Johnston and Fort Caswell realized they could not defend them. The forts were abandoned. As they left Fort Caswell, the troops bombed or burned several parts of the fort. Caswell troops joined the men from Fort Johnston and wearily marched to Fort Anderson at Brunswick for the next stand against the enemy. The Federal troops occupied Smithville and began efforts to reach Wilmington. The same Lt. Cushing who had made the daring raid on the town in February 1864 was still anchored off Fort Caswell aboard the *Monticello*. In a letter dated January 31, 1865, Cushing wrote to Admiral Porter describing the surrender of Smithville. (Appendix C).

Lt. Cushing was named military governor of Smithville and chose as his headquarters General Hebert's house. While he and other officers relaxed, the sailors were roaming the town creating problems and committing acts of vandalism. Breaking into the courthouse, the sailors destroyed many valuable papers. They vandalized the Masonic Lodge on Nash Street and stole the jewel of the order. However, their ship's surgeon was a Mason, and he forced them to return the jewel. The town's people felt blessed when the naval men were replaced by the 149th New York Regiment, a well-disciplined Army unit.

On April 26, 1865, the final terms of the Confederate surrender were declared, and except for a few scattered skirmishes, the war was over. Gloom settled over Smithville as the citizens realized "the cause" had been lost and their future was uncertain. They wept openly and silently for their men who had died so tragically.

As the citizens tried to adjust to the new order of living, St. Philip's Chapel was seized and occupied by Federal troops as a hospital for the sick and wounded. Later it was used as a school for freed blacks. The Union soldiers conducted a search throughout the town collecting firearms found in the homes. Resentment was strong in the hearts of the people; tempers often flared between them and the troops stationed at the fort.

In July 1865 the Freedmen's Bureau began operating for the blacks in North Carolina to provide food, shelter, and clothing; to give medical treatment; and to provide education to help prepare them for the future. Negotiating assistance was given in working out labor contracts. One of the units was set up on Bald Head Island and another at Fort Anderson. Most of the negotiating was done by Union soldiers who had little sympathy or concern for the freedmen. Some civilians, locally called "carpetbaggers", worked with the soldiers. The best work was done, throughout the South, by female school teachers sent out by Northern church mission societies to provide education for black children.

More than 40,000 North Carolinians had died at war or in prison camps. State and local governments had collapsed, and the main source of labor, slavery, had disappeared. Banks were closing; many of the schools and colleges closed with little hope of re-opening. Many people had lost their homes, livestock, and personal belongings. Military rule was in effect until the end of 1865.

Damages in Smithville were not as severe as in many places. The people were able to maintain their gardens and to grow much of their needed food. Fish, oysters, and clams were readily available. Coffee, sugar, and flour were in short supply, but inhabitants made do with what they had. One of the hardest things to obtain was cloth for clothing; shoes were also scarce. Resourcefulness was stretched to the limit as people lived by the maxim "use it up, make it do, and do without." This philosophy was still felt by the next generation following the war.

Reconstruction—a period of bitterness, violence, and tragedy—began for the South in March 1867 when Congress passed the Reconstruction Act. North Carolina became a part of Military District Number 2 until July of 1868. The regular state government could operate, but disputes were handled by the Major General of the District.

Life in Smithville moved smoothly in spite of a few major flareups between the citizens, the soldiers at the fort, and the Union loyalists. When General William T. Sherman left North Carolina after the last major battle of the Civil War at Appomattox, General John M. Schofield was put in charge of military rule in North Carolina. Schofield arranged for each county to have a police force, manned by local officials who had favored the Union. This, of course, set the stage for the conflicts that soon came.

As early as 1866 business began to revive in Brunswick County and the Cape Fear area. Large quantities of rosin and turpentine were produced and shipped from Wilmington. Cotton was again cultivated and taken to Wilmington for transportation. All of this affected business in Smithville. The wharves on the waterfront accommodated all kinds of sailing vessels making stopovers on their way to and from Wilmington. The sandy streets were crowded with river pilots, sailors, and local fishermen. Business was brisk at taverns and boarding houses along Bay Street and the water's edge. Congress extended the work of the Freedmen's Bureau until the end of 1868 and the basic needs of blacks were met. Many black women found employment as cooks or laundresses in the homes where they had once been slaves. Their wages were meager and life very hard. During this period of the town's history many blacks gathered into a little community in the western part of the town.

In March 1866 civil government was restored in Brunswick County. Twelve justices of the peace were commissioned by the governor; they met regularly at the Smithville courthouse for the Court of Pleas and Quarter Sessions. A sheriff and several other officers were elected and took office. One of the sheriff's first court orders was to round-up records which had been removed for safe-keeping before the war and return them to the courthouse in Smithville.

The court also contracted for repairs to the war-damaged courthouse.

In the spring of 1868, North Carolina adopted a new, federally-approved constitution and was re-admitted to the Union in July. This constitution provided for a new system of county government with townships as the local government units, much like the township system in New England. In 1876, generally conceded to be the end of the Reconstruction Period, the General Assembly changed this form of county government. Geographically the never popular townships remained the same, but they had no governmental powers.

In July 1868, Fourth of July celebrations resumed in Smithville with excursions and boat races. A band played and salutes were fired from Fort Johnston by the U.S. 6th Infantry. Hostilities between the townspeople and the government troops had subsided, and friendships were formed. In September 1869 a terrible fire broke out on the Smithville waterfront. Much damage was done before the flames were brought under control, but soldiers from the fort and sailors from river vessels fought valiantly with the citizens to salvage what they could.

During this same period an incident occurred that brought Miss Kate Stuart national fame and the title *Heroine of Smithville*. Miss Stuart had agreed to keep the little daughter of Captain Alex Hunter of Clyde Lines for the day. The child was playing on the porch under Miss Kate's watchful eye. When little Mary saw her father's ship passing in front of the house she darted off the porch, and out on the dock to wave to her father who was on the ship's deck waving. In her eagerness, the child ran off the end of the dock. Miss Kate, long skirts and all, flew to the rescue, grabbed the child, and held her with one hand and the dock with the other until help could arrive. Captain Hunter, witnessing the entire incident, spread the fame of Miss Stuart and later gave her a gold watch inscribed to express his gratitude. As long as the Clyde Lines operated on the lower Cape Fear, each ship gave a salute to Miss Kate upon passing the Stuart House.

As Smithville entered the new decade, the town had grown and business had improved greatly. Reflecting that growth, local leaders felt that town limits should be extended and in February 1870 introduced a bill in the General Assembly to allow the expansion. The bill passed in March after several readings. Although no map is available to show the exact limits, the town began to develop in both a northerly and westerly direction.

The 1870 Federal Census showed the village of Smithville with 133 houses, 151 families, and a total population of 810 persons. Most of the listed occupations were related to the river. The Revenue Cutter *Seward* stationed at Fort Johnston had twelve men as officers and crew. Other occupations given were merchants, cabinet makers, a brick mason, blacksmith, jail keeper, machinist, two physicians, a "ginger beer maker," and three schoolteachers.

In July of 1870, a Wilmington newspaper had this to say about Smithville:

> *Smithville is said to be unusually pleasant this season. Why don't our people spend their summers there instead of running off to Virginia Springs?*

In December there was a government release describing the structures on the Fort Johnston reservation. It stated that there was no fort but there was a barracks building, a kitchen with messroom, a laundry building, the officers quarters, office building, the old blockhouse which was being used as a warehouse, the guardhouse, hospital, "dead house," bakery, and stable. The bathhouse was on the river beach and the release stated, "The men bathe daily in the summer." (With so many structures in so small a space, it is no wonder that about twenty years later the town citizens were demanding that the reservation be cleared of many unsightly buildings and fences.) At the end of the document it says there was a six-acre post garden located a half-mile from the fort.

As another indication of town growth, Baptists living in Smithville decided to organize and build a church. Most of them were members of Bethel Baptist Church, a short distance from town. Mr. John L. Wescott, local merchant and a Bethel member, donated money to build a meeting house and construction started in March 1871. By September the building, located on the corners of Nash and Howe Streets, was ready for occupancy. George R. French and Philip Heinsberger of Wilmington, business friends of John L. Wescott, gave the first bell and first minute book to the new congregation. The original thirteen charter members have grown to more than 800 church members today.

That same spring, the Wilmington and Smithville Steamboat Company was incorporated. Four Smithville men were among those named as directors of the company: Thomas G. Drew, Captain W. J. Potter, John H. Thees, and Dr. Walter G. Curtis. In July it was noted that all the boarding houses were filled and there were plans to build more boarding houses to take care of the expected crowds of summer visitors.

In December the St. James AME Zion Church was organized. Mrs. Sarah Cotton, a founder who lived to be over 100 years-old, had a quiet, hardworking life and was highly respected by all who knew her. The first church building was made from the frame of the old quarantine hospital moved from the beach near Deep Water Point. Today's church, a brick structure, stands at the corner of West and Rhett Streets.

In February 1872 fire totally destroyed two houses and other buildings on Water Street (probably today's Bay Street). The lack of fire fighting equipment contributed to the amount of destruction. The fire gave new importance to a movement to convince town officials of the necessity of having "at least one good fire engine."

The Brunswick County Commissioners, at the request of the townspeople, sent a petition to Governor Tod Caldwell and to the Military Commander at Fort Johnston. This petition, directed toward the Army who deprived the local citizens the use of Ellis Street and parts of Moore and Bay Streets, asked to have these streets opened for public use.

In 1873 the U.S. Government made plans to establish life saving stations along the coast at Oak Island and on Bald Head Island creating employment for many of Smithville's men. When completed, the stations were furnished with surf boats, mortars for throwing line, life cars, custom lights, rockets, and flags for signaling.

In the summer of 1873, a Wilmington newspaper stated:

> *Among the attractions in Smithville, not the least is Captain Rosafy's bath houses for ladies and gentlemen. They are fitted up in excellent style, and are a great comfort to the denizens of that locality. This is an institution which should be liberally patronized.*

Captain Rosafy, operator of what he termed a "hotel" on the waterfront, had come to the area as a carpetbagger after the Civil War. He was appointed inspector of customs at Smithville, but was soon under investigation for his conduct. Rosafy was removed from the office and was succeeded by Robert M. Wescott until, two years later, he was reinstated to the position. Earlier as justice of the peace, Rosafy was sent to jail for unlawful seizure of property. In the years that followed, his record is peppered with incidents of false imprisonment, forcible trespass, and political rally brawls. Even so, he was nominated by Brunswick County Republicans to represent Brunswick and New Hanover Counties in the state legislature.

Through the fall of 1873, the village was battling a diphtheria epidemic that claimed the lives of many young children. Small stones in the Old Smithville Burying Ground give mute evidence to the sorrow felt by the families.

The next spring a move was begun to clear the Cape Fear River channel and deepen the water over the bar to enhance commercial shipping from the outside world to the Wilmington port. The river was often filled with many-sized vessels as they stopped at Smithville wharves for supplies and to leave cargo for the small waterfront businesses.

The summer was filled with the usual activities of boat races, excursions, picnics, and "sea bathing" near Captain Rosafy's new bathhouses. In celebration of Independence Day, the men stationed at Fort Johnston held a fireworks display "to benefit the various churches in town."

The summer of 1875 saw Colonel William P. Craighill of the U.S. Corps of Engineers in Smithville accepting proposals for the closing of New Inlet. This closure (done by a New York firm) further increased the depth of the Cape Fear from Smithville to Wilmington. Colonel Craighill remained in Smithville for many years supervising this unusually difficult engineering project that was not officially considered complete until 1881. Assisting with the supervision of the work was Captain Henry Bacon, who also lived in Smithville. Bacon's son, Francis, became a well-known architect, and another son, Henry, Jr., designed the Lincoln Memorial in Washington, D.C. Francis Bacon, in a letter dated 1876, wrote to a friend telling of his days as a youth in Smithville:

We got up amateur theatricals. I painted the scenery and was stage manager. It was nice to be with my family again. My little brother Carl a baby born in 1876 just before I arrived. Younger children, George, Harry and Lucy. Kate and Jim at school in the North. Father had a cat-boat, the Dolly, to use in his work and I enjoyed sailing about in the soft warm

Southern air. Dr. Curtis, a keen musician with his harmonium,
I with flute—we loved the Mozart Violin sonatas. Up and down
river to Wilmington in the government tug. Captain Harper,
and a black cook who got us tasty meals.

The village began receiving daily mail service in the summer of
1875. The Wilmington Morning Star announced:

The daily mail to Smithville will begin July 1. We think Mr.
O.G. Parsley will be the contractor and the quick little steamer
Dixie will be the mail boat.

July 4th of that summer saw the townspeople gaily celebrating
as usual. There were the time-honored boat races, excursions, and
the firing of cannon and guns. All the church bells in town rang
out, a parade marched through the streets, and all the ships in port
flew their flags. In the evening, a fireworks display was held from
the wharf of the Stuart House.

Baseball was the favored game of Smithville for a number of
years. In 1877 there were two ball clubs, the *Rangers* manned by
town citizens, and the *Meteors*, whose membership was composed
of soldiers. The championship was won by the *Rangers* with a ten
point lead.

On April 12, 1877, a tragedy occurred. The pilot boats *Mary K.*
Sprunt and *Uriah Timmons* were caught at sea in a terrible storm
which raged for three days. The *Mary K. Sprunt*, her 39-year-old
captain Thomas B. Grissom, and his entire crew of young men,
Robert S. Walker, C.C. Pinner, Charles Dosher, and Lawrence
Gillespie, were lost. In spite of the ferocity of the storm and because
of the heroism of Joseph Arnold, the only unmarried crew member,
who volunteered to undertake the dangerous mission to cut the
jib-halliard, the *Uriah Timmons* made it to Georgetown, S.C. with
its courageous four-man crew (C.C. Morse, Julius Weeks, Joseph
Thompson, Jr., and Joseph Arnold) weary but safe.

Two years later, a still-grieving citizenry and the Cape Fear Pilots
Association erected a grand obelisk monument in the Smithville
Burying Ground in memory of the pilots drowned in the 1877 storm
and five other pilots who drowned in a storm on December 11, 1872.
On a beautiful day in May, with great ceremony and a flowery
oratory, the monument was dedicated. The N.C. Commissioners
of Navigation and Pilotage were special guests, a minister from

Wilmington gave the oration, and music was furnished by the choir of Wilmington's Front Street Methodist Church. Dr. Walter G. Curtis, Cape Fear Quarantine Officer and influential citizen of Smithville, was master of ceremonies.

This cenotaph erected by friends and relatives stands at the southeast corner of Smithville Burial Ground as a memorial to two groups of pilots who died in shipwrecks in the 19th century.

A Town Renamed—
A Time of Progress
1878-1899

Smithville emerged from the Reconstruction Period showing progress and growth. From the tiny sleepy resort and fishing village centering on Fort Johnston, Smithville had become a town.

The tenth Federal Census showed that Brunswick County's population, just under 9,400, was divided almost equally between black and white citizens. Of that population, Smithville had 204 families for a total occupancy of 1,025—more than double that of ten years before. Again the listed occupations showed dependence upon the river for the livelihood of most residents. Thirteen men were listed as U.S. Government employees working on the lightship, the revenue cutter, in the customs service, on the government dredge in the harbor, and as signal officer at U.S. Signal Station. The census also showed that sixty-two people were living at Fort Johnston.

In December 1880, rumor was that Fort Johnston would be abandoned in the near future. The citizens were upset because Fort Johnston had been essential to the town since its very earliest days. Their protests availed nothing however, and in February Major Graves and his detachment of Second U.S. Artillery, comprising the garrison at the fort, departed for Washington, D.C. Graves left behind Lt. Niels and two enlisted men as caretakers of Fort Johnston.

Emmanuel Garcia, born to Portuguese parents on April 13, 1854, in the Azore Islands, arrived in Smithville in 1881 and became widely known as a master boatbuilder. Due to their common Portuguese background, Garcia became good friends with Andrew Bowers. Bowers, who lived on Bald Head Island with his family during the Civil War, had moved to Smithville. Emmanuel Garcia purchased a lot on Nash Street and built a small residence there in 1884. Three years later his friend Bowers died and the following year Garcia married the widow Bowers. In 1893 the couple sold their Nash Street home and built a larger one on Bay Street before they moved to Wilmington in 1896. There he established the Garcia Shipyard which built many vessels widely known for their beauty and expert workmanship. In 1901, Emmanuel Garcia died of "consumption" and was buried in Wilmington's Oakdale Cemetery. In 1924 his widow, Mary Jane, a native of Smithville, also died.

In the summer of 1882 newspapers noted that crowds of townspeople and summer residents were frequenting the Hotel Brunswick where "twelve to fifteen couples" danced at nightly dances in the ballroom. Pasquale Pascucci's band from Wilmington frequently provided the music. Once a band of harpists were engaged to provide entertainment at the hotel. On the afternoon before the scheduled concert one of the harpists, Antonio Casseletta, known to his friends as "Tony", went sailing on the Cape Fear. After his boat capsized and sank, Tony's body was recovered and buried in the Smithville Cemetery. Legend says that even now his spirit roams through the Brunswick Inn (sometimes called Hotel Brunswick—now the Arrington-Callari home) looking for his harp. His wife and child survived him in Wilmington.

Smithville's fame as a resort town spread when, in August 1883, a Charlotte, N.C. newspaper wrote:

> From Long Branch, N.J. to Savannah, Georgia . . . there is no superior location as a sea-side resort than Smithville, N.C. . . . With the ocean in full view from the hotel verandah, with steamers and sailing vessels nearly always passing to and from Wilmington . . . we know of no more pleasant place than Smithville.

But "pleasant Smithville" also knew the fury of storm, earthquake, and fire. One month after the newspaper article, a devastating hurricane hit the coast near Smithville, with maximum winds of 93 miles-per-hour and sustained winds of 81 miles-per-hour that blew for seven hours. Fences and lightly constructed buildings were destroyed and considerable crop damage was experienced throughout the area. Many beautiful, old trees were uprooted while leaves on the standing trees appeared frostbitten due to the driving salt spray. Telegraph lines were blown down and many vessels, including the *Frying Pan Lightship*, broke from their moorings and were driven ashore. Thirty-three passengers from the disabled steamer *City of Atlanta* were rescued by the Revenue Cutter *Cofax* and the steamer was towed into Smithville when the storm subsided.

In August 1885 another hurricane came ashore near Smithville. Winds were recorded at 98 miles-per-hour in the late afternoon before the anemometer was blown away. Within the next half hour, the winds reached an estimated 125 miles-per-hour. Every house on the waterfront suffered roof damage with total estimated damages in Smithville over $100,000. Boats were blown ashore and trees again suffered great damage. An October hurricane caused less damage than the one in August but brought high tides that "submerged the entire waterfront." The old-timers declared that this tide was the highest in ten years.

Also in October, a fire caused considerable damage as it spread to several houses on the waterfront. A bucket brigade from the river to the home of *Colfax* pilot E.H. Cranmer saved his residence. Fires were often reported, and the bucket brigade was the only means of saving buildings.

Less than a year later the Signal Corps officer at Smithville reported:

A severe earthquake shock felt here at 9:50 p.m., lasted ten seconds, came from the northwest. Ten minutes after the first shock another came from the west, lasting about three seconds.

The earthquake from which these shocks were felt was centered at Charleston, S.C. and has since been called "the Charleston earthquake." In September more tremors were experienced in Smithville, but there was no damage except from abnormally high tides. In November, just as residents settled back to normal, another earthquake shock was felt. Although there was no appreciable damage to property, the citizens were alarmed and ran into the streets seeking consolation from each other.

When not coping with fires, hurricanes, or a possible earthquake, there were ever-increasing discussions and rumors about the possibility of a railroad in town. This railroad would serve its citizens and also create a port and coaling station in Smithville. Intentions were announced by several groups, but over and over came the disheartening news of abandoned plans.

Some people never gave up. Smithville's newspapers continued to play a strong role in keeping the issue alive while striving to stay alive themselves. Most publishing efforts in town had a short lifespan. Each newspaper, while in existence, championed progress and encouraged civic leaders to "Go Forward," as one editor-publisher often said. Local news was printed weekly along with national and international news copied from northern newspapers. Most of the advertising was from Wilmington merchants.

The town population kept growing. Business activity increased, more houses were built, and the public school enrollment was larger each year, even though there were also at least two private schools. As the town grew so did the interest in a railroad. The Northern and Southern Railroad Company, incorporated by the 1886 legislature, planned for a railroad from Wilmington to Smithville and rented part of the Pavilion, located at the foot of Potts Street (now Atlantic Avenue), for its offices. Anticipation was in the air once again.

The new railroad company planned to build wharves near the Pavilion. The developers, envisioning a port that would be the largest in the south, rivaling Norfolk and Charleston - requested that the town name be changed to "Southport" to draw attention to "the Port of the South."

Town leaders, eager to please the company that promised a railroad and a port, asked their Raleigh representative to enter the necessary legislation. On March 4, 1887, the bill was enacted, and the name of Smithville was changed to Southport (Appendix D). On May 29, 1887, Postmaster W.R. Ferguson gave official notice that the name of the town and post office had been changed to Southport.

Almost immediately, the Southport Improvement Club was organized with Dr. Walter G. Curtis as president, M.C. Guthrie as secretary, and S.P. Tharp as treasurer. All three were public-minded citizens who wished to see the town grow. One week later the newspaper reported that people were "sprucing up" the town. There was increased business activity, several houses were under construction, and many visitors were coming to town each day. At one time, twenty people found lodging in the Pavilion, where the railroad offices were located, as the hotels were all filled.

The summer visitors and townspeople alike were finding it difficult to use the new town name. Many of the businesses' names also had to be changed. Members of the Smithville Baptist Church, organized in 1871, did not change the church's name for five years.

The "salubrious breezes" that had enticed Joshua Potts to start the town continued to enchant the visitors. Most of the porches were double-galleried, and they made great places for socializing and whiling away the summer hours on joggle boards, porch swings and rocking chairs. For the men inclined toward conversation and philosophy, there was the "Whittlers Bench" at the foot of Howe Street where they, too, could catch the breeze. While they whittled and talked, they kept their eyes on the harbor activity and anxiously anticipated Southport becoming a large river port.

Whittlers Bench.

The "Whittlers Bench" origin has caused many tales and legends to evolve. The best documented sources say it was established about 1888 by S. Paxton "Pack" Tharp when a bench was built around two cedar trees at the foot of Howe Street where men gathered to pass the time and to talk politics. Sometimes, as the discussions grew heated, the men whittled furiously often cutting the cedar bench. Other times they brought their own sticks of wood for carving. Whittling or wood carving was a custom dating back to early colonial times and those who whittled were carrying on their fathers' tradition. The cedar trees were sometimes named for politicians or men who made news. Some of those so honored were William Jennings Bryan, Clarence Darrow, William McKinley, Woodrow Wilson, Bill Bryan, and Warren Harding. Other "Whittlers Bench" tales say that enough corn liquor was drunk there to float a battleship and that a nearby store sold two or three gross of knives every week.

Continued talk around the "Whittlers Bench" and among the city officials centered around the proposed railroad. Over a period of several years, seven attempts had been made by various companies to establish a railroad to Smithville/Southport, but these efforts always seemed to fade away. It was not until 1911 that an attempt became a reality.

However, with the talk of a railroad and a port, the town officials in August 1887 authorized improvements to the sandy streets. A few days later town workers were laying crushed oyster shells on the streets. The town minutes show purchases of many bushels of oyster shells for this purpose. Meanwhile, other workers cleared bushes and undergrowth in undeveloped areas where streets were planned. Public subscriptions helped pay for these projects.

Captain John W. Woodside, master of the steam dredge *Woodbury*, was busily engaged in deepening and straightening the channel in anticipation of expected commercial development. Retailers Guthrie and Ruark completed a new store with a plate glass front at the corner of Moore and Lord Streets. Drew and Davis, retailers also, completed their new store on Dry Street.

May 1888 was a busy month in Southport. Captain John W. Harper, a strong supporter of growth and improvement, purchased the *Sylvan Grove*. This double side-wheeled vessel was to run from Wilmington to Carolina Beach and on to Southport. Harper's pilot boat, the *Louise*, was repaired and made ready for the summer season. Captain Richard Dosher and a Mr. Wiggs purchased the 72-foot steamer *Bessie*, which could carry 75 passengers, to run between Wilmington and Southport with passengers and mail.

A strong rivalry developed between the owners of excursion and pilot boats. This was especially true when a Florida excursion boat,

Queen of St. Johns, with a 1,500 passenger capacity, attempted to capture a share of the business. Miss Kate Stuart got into the fray by allowing Captain J.G. Christopher, owner of the *Queen*, to build a wharf in front of her boarding house. In addition, he also built a wharf and bathing house at Fort Caswell. To counteract Christopher's efforts, Captain John W. Harper built a Fort Caswell dock for his steamers, and Captain James T. Harper built a wharf for his newly purchased tug boat. The *Queen of St. Johns* had an unprofitable season and was moored near Wilmington for the 1888 winter. She was destroyed by fire the following July giving the men at the "Whittlers Bench" a great deal to talk about.

The congregation of the Methodist Church felt the need for a larger building and the Conference voted unanimously for the new "edifice." By September 1888 they laid the cornerstone with a ceremony led by the Grand Lodge of Masons of North Carolina. The 34 by 55 foot frame structure was designed by B.L. Price, a Philadelphia architect. While construction was underway, worship services were held in the courthouse across the street. Several successful fund-raising events were held for the new church building.

In his book, *The Architecture of Southport*, noted architectural historian Carl Lounsbury states:

> *Completed in May 1890, the new Methodist Episcopal Church, South, set in a spacious surrounding, is the best testament to the imagination and competent skills of native Southport carpenter-builders, working in the Victorian Gothic . . . Messrs. Fore and Foster of Wilmington designed and made the stain glass for the lancet windows . . . Highly polished Carolina pine is employed for the interior finish.*

Henry Daniel directed the construction over a two-year period. Much of the labor was donated, bringing the cost of the church under $3,500. The original frame church was moved to North Lord Street and renovated by the black Methodists, pastored by Rev. Whitfield Griffin.

With civic improvement still the order of the day, many of the dilapidated buildings on the Fort Johnston reservation were sold at prices ranging from $12 to $150. Several of the structures were bought by leading contractor A.J. Robbins and moved to other locations in town. Many were converted into residences or attached to existing residences for added living space. The largest wooden structure moved was the hospital standing at the eastern edge of the reservation. This building was moved to a bluff overlooking the river at 413 East Bay Street; a one-story bay window was added on the western side and a small two-story bay was attached on the eastern side. In addition, a new one-story front porch was added before the structure was sold to Captain Thomas Morse who subsequently sold it to Jens Berg. Years later, Ed Swain, who helped Mr. Robbins move the house, made an affidavit for Miss Annie May Woodside who inherited the house from her stepfather Jens Berg. This affidavit stated that the Woodside home had once been the main part of the 1808 Fort Hospital moved by Mr. Robbins to its present location. Miss Woodside lived in this house until her death in 1981. Presently the house is owned by Dr. and Mrs. Sidney Fortney.

With the removal of the buildings from the reservation, the town planned to make a public park on the site. Benches were placed on the grass so people could watch the vessels in the harbor, enjoy the breezes, and rest or socialize. Sometimes a community organization would have an ice cream supper on the Garrison lawn where, for a small amount, one could delight in a dish of homemade ice cream and a slice of real pound cake. At other times the town ladies would set up their wares on the lawns in front of their own homes to raise money for their favorite benefit. Many dollars for churches and clubs were raised in this manner.

Some years before, a hurricane had carved a gully near the Garrison along Bay Street. As part of the general improvement plan, a small wooden bridge was built across the ravine connecting Bay Street with the Fort Johnston grounds. A bench was placed on one side of the bridge creating a convenient spot for moonlight gatherings and romance.

Also during the time of general improvements, a town meeting was called to discuss street signage and additional sidewalks. To further indicate their desire for progress, the citizens petitioned their county representative for an act to incorporate the Town of Southport into the City of Southport which was done in April 1889.

In July, E.B. Stevens, a member of the Chicago Board of Trade, was traveling in North Carolina attempting to keep alive plans and dreams to build another railroad. The route of this one was from Bristol, Tennessee to Southport. All of the many previous efforts had failed, including the recent Northern and Southern Railway.

In November the surveying team of the Cape Fear and Cincinnati Railway Company had come to mark a line between Southport and Wilmington.

On February 27, 1890, the first issue of the *Southport Leader*, edited by Chicago transplant C.L. Stevens, son of E. B. Stevens, came off the press. The twenty-four column paper's subscription rate was one dollar a year. The *Southport Leader* truly became a leader as an advocate and promoter of business and civic affairs of the city. Through the newspaper pages, Editor Stevens undertook a town census with the results showing a population of 1,181, an 18% increase over the 1880 Federal Census. Fortunately this census was taken because most of the Federal Census of 1890 was destroyed by fire.

The *Leader* called attention to things of interest going on in town. The Cape Fear Cornet Band, with Samuel Drew as manager and band leader, had eleven members who practiced once a week. Edward H. Cranmer, Jr. was secretary and Asa Dosher was treasurer of this organization. About the same time there was the Silver Cornet Band led by Professor Schloss. Each of these bands gave concerts; the Silver Cornet Band even played for a moonlight excursion from Wilmington to Southport as a benefit for the Oxford Orphanage. As this was the era known as the *Golden Age of Brass Bands*, no town could pretend to have progressed unless it had at least one brass band. Southport was not about to be left out.

Although the Fourth of July celebration was several months away, the *Leader* was announcing the 1890 festival plans. The annual Southport Regatta was to be held as usual, and the paper stated:

> *Among the many races, sail and rowing, the most exciting will be the sailing contest for the "Leader's Cup" (the cup of course to be awarded by the newspaper). The leading business houses of Southport will add lesser prizes to be contested for and the day will be one full of interest to lovers of marine sports.*

Also noted in the same issue was that:

> *The Southport schools were never in as good condition as at present. The Academy with new furniture offers pleasant surroundings and most efficient teachers in all branches, and the excellent private schools of Mr. T.J. Wescott, Miss Theodocia Prigge, and Miss Fannie Price offer additional facilities for all.*

According to the *Leader*, "the west end of the city" was experiencing a building boom with three houses under construction and several others undergoing renovations and improvements. Refurbishment of properties on the "east side" were also noted. "These improvements will stimulate others and we will have to record other buildings soon."

At a local grocery store, a housewife could buy a half-bushel of sweet potatoes, a peck of Irish potatoes, a one-third bushel of cornmeal, a bushel of peas, three dozen eggs, five pounds of pork and bacon, five pounds of beef, three chickens, six flounders, eight sheepshead, 32 mullets, eight blackfish, and three dozen small crabs for $7.45. Naturally, with all these supplies she was probably running one of the boarding houses on Bay or Moore Street. It would take two grocery boys to help her take the goods home.

When the Fourth of July arrived, it was billed as a "regular old-fashioned Fourth of July celebration." Along with marine sports, there were the usual orations, music by the Cape Fear Cornet Band, and singing by 42 ladies representing the states of the union. The fireworks were set-off from Battery Island, mindful that fire was an ever-present danger in Southport due to little firefighting equipment. The single women fared well in July as twenty-eight South Carolina militia men of the Marion Rifles, Fourth Regiment arrived for a ten-day encampment. The ten-piece Marion Rifle Band also accompanied the group. During their encampment, many dances and other entertainments were held.

A coaling dock opened for business, a canning factory was established, and railroad hopes were once again raised by more "promises." The Evergreen Park and Cemetery Company was chartered. This new cemetery was planned for ten acres of land outside the city limits, but was finally abandoned when the promoters could not raise enough capital for the project.

As the decade ended the *Leader* declared:

> *A gentleman who visited Southport yesterday for the first time in several years, tells us some of his impressions. He says that he had heard considerable of the improvements but did not expect to find so many. He was much struck with the appearance of the little town, greatly improved as it had been in recent years. He says that the enterprising citizens of the town have got improvements on the brain and it is the order of the day now.*

There is still much railroad talk and hopes that Southport will eventually become the terminus of a great system.

Entering the last decade of the nineteenth century, more Southport businesses were established. Twelve boats gathered oysters and clams for shipment to northern markets. Soon the Southport Construction Company was organized and a lumber mill began transactions. Yet another charter was granted for two railroad companies who felt that there was plenty of business for them. A fishing company opened at Fort Caswell with one boat, a ten-man crew, and a beach camp. In one day they hauled in forty-two bushels of fish.

On February 26, 1891, the "city lamps" were placed in position and lit. Also during the early "gay 90s," a northwestern subdivision known as "the Cottage Place" was developed by W.B. Stevens on recently platted town lands. Brunswick Street, known as "Tin Pan Alley" or "the Alley," was widened and more houses were built along it. Other sections of town boasted five new houses under construction. Dr. D.I. Watson, a popular physician and druggist, was elected mayor (Appendix E).

Before the year's end, the county seat controversy was raised again. In September, an "exciting meeting" of the county magistrates was held at the courthouse and the majority present "designated Lockwood's Folly as the place to which the county buildings shall be moved." Although this action sparked a lot of opposition in Southport and other county areas, a fund raising drive for the move was undertaken. The editor of the *Leader* avidly opposed the move in several editorials. He pointed out that such action would not benefit the people in general. He wisely stated that, "A few court days does not make an interior point a city." Another argument was that because Southport was on the verge of becoming a great port, the county seat should remain there. Nevertheless, the General Assembly approved a $7,000 bond issue to finance the move and ordered another election on the subject. Because of disagreements among officials, the election was not held until early 1892. When the votes were counted, those opposing the move had won by a large majority. The matter was finished, and rivalry among the communities in the growing county continued. Sixty-five years later, the county seat was actually moved from Southport.

The city's centennial year passed without fanfare or mention, which is strange for a town so given to celebration. One of the biggest news item for the year was that rare plants had been found on Bald Head Island. Samples were collected in large tubs filled with native soil and were shipped by rail to the Chicago World's Fair. Four large palmetto trees were shipped a month later for exhibition there also.

About the same time, the Post Office Department decided to have mail between Southport and Wilmington carried on horseback instead of by steamer. The horseback trip consumed ten hours instead of the three hours by water. Citizens were furious and soon the mail was again traveling on the Cape Fear.

Dr. Walter Curtis, the quarantine physician, recommended to the North Carolina Board of Health that a quarantine hospital be built. Previously he was required to board each vessel and make an inspection. Curtis was accommodating anyone removed from the ships in a small, four-room facility at Deep Water Point. The port of Wilmington was growing rapidly and daily traffic by ships was increasing accordingly. With the little structure so close to town, citizens were apprehensive about the possible spread of the prevalent communicable diseases—smallpox, yellow fever, and tuberculosis. At Dr. Curtis' invitation, the North Carolina Board of Health was entertained by Dr. and Mrs. Curtis at a meeting in Southport. The board agreed that a quarantine hospital was needed, but no action was taken for several years.

Between the 1890 Federal Census and 1893, Southport's population increased to 1,390, as revealed in another survey by the *Leader*. Early in 1893 eight houses were built, and the Cape Fear Harbor and Coal Company was chartered. However, the best news came on January 21st when Mayor R.M. Wescott announced the purchase of a hook-and-ladder truck from the Wilmington Fire Department with delivery promised within ten days. The stable of A.J. Robbins, located at the foot of Boundary (now Caswell) Street, was to be the truck's temporary station. A permanent home for the equipment was to be built by Henry Daniel at the rear of the city jail. Less than two weeks later a hook-and-ladder company of twenty volunteers was organized. The citizenry was elated about the fire company because the possibility of fire damage was always present in Southport.

Interest in education continued. A.E. Stevens headed a drive to establish a free library and reading room. The Sweet Violet Band staged a benefit for this cause. The result is unknown, but years later Mr. Stevens' sister, Jessie Stevens Taylor, spearheaded another movement for a library which was very successful. As a result, today we have three libraries in Brunswick County Library System, with two others in the development stages.

Oystering was the way to make a living for many in Southport. About twenty-five boats were employed in the trade with the cannery buying all oysters gathered. Several small schooners were engaged in carrying oyster shells to Wilmington for use on their streets. At one point forty thousand bushels had been delivered, and there was still a demand.

Dr. Curtis' wife, Margaret, and two of their children left Wilmington by Atlantic Coast Line Railroad at 9:30 a.m. on August 20th for a trip to Chicago to visit friends and see the World's Fair. Dr. Curtis could not leave his medical practice and his quarantine duties, especially since his request for a new hospital was still under consideration. As revealed in her diary, faithfully kept from November 1886 until October 1896, Mrs. Curtis was not always happy living in Southport after having spent most of her life in larger northern cities. Sometimes she felt she had to get away from it, and taking her young sons to the World's Fair gave her a wonderful excuse to do so. Of the fair she said:

> *It is impossible of conception before seeing it, and almost beyond comparison after going through it. Ten years of travel would not give so adequate an idea of the habits, customs, and works of foreign nations as can be had here in a day or two.*

The boys were excitedly enjoying the whole adventure. A week later a diary entry recorded:

> *Sun. the 27th of Aug. 1893 was beautiful in Chicago. We went to church. But how different at home in Southport where they were having the most terrific storm that has ever been known on the coast, and lasted two days and nights wrecking vessels by the scores and emense loss of life. Fifteen hundred are said to have been drowned on the sea islands. Beaufort, S. C., Charleston was badly injured; Southport not at all.*

Mrs. Curtis and the children returned home in a few days and six weeks later she made another storm entry in her diary on October 13, 1893:

The storm is indeed upon us in all its fury; nothing has ever equaled it here. All night the wind shrieked and wailed; then like a great rush of waters; we were up and down most of the night. It increased dreadfully all the morning until the tide rose far higher than ever known before. All the wharfs went, one after the other; and every building on the beach, custom house and all, went, except the pavilion, that was not at all injured. It looked very dreadful to see the buildings go down one by one, then entirely break up. The waves were enormous and like the ocean; tossed great timbers like kindling wood. The pilot boat Addie was tossed high and dry on the beach. The wind was blowing at 103 miles an hour. Walter had to go out; could hardly keep his footing. About four o'clock the wind shifted to the west, and the sea went down rapidly. At five o'clock the wind went down so much we went over to Miss Kate Stuart's to see the condition of things. Her yard a mass of debris; and large quantity of lumber, everything washed away up to the porch; and that almost down. It was a distressing sight. We then went through the Garrison, and all was destruction as far as one could see. The waves washed entirely over Oak Island from the ocean; water poured through the lighthouse; so the keeper's wife had to be carried waist-deep to the high sand hills near. It made great changes over there. All quiet tonight.

Years later in 1962, the U.S. Department of Commerce published a report entitled *North Carolina Hurricanes: A Descriptive Listing of Tropical Cyclones Which Have Affected the State*. This report described this October 13, 1893 storm as being similar to Hurricane Hazel in 1954.

The highest reported wind in North Carolina was 94 miles-per-hour at Southport . . . the tide and overflow of water were reported as the highest known to date, being 16 inches above the highwater mark of 1893. Great damage was reported to forest, crops and property.

The day following the 1893 storm, Mrs. Curtis made this entry:

A perfectly beautiful day, no one would imagine the old river had been behaving so badly, so smooth and dimpled with smiles now. Nothing so treacherous as water. The wrecks are beginning to come in, and it is dreadful to see them.

71

The next year brought happier and more peaceful times. The North Carolina Naval Reservists came in April and again in August for their annual training, and the young women in Southport were especially delighted. One seaman was reportedly "hopelessly in love with several of Southport's prettiest girls." Mrs. Curtis acknowledged "a bustle about the town which is very agreeable."

The Civil War monitor *Nantucket*, manned by the Wilmington Division of the Naval Reserves, was at Southport for ten days and was joined by the modern cruiser *Montgomery* with her crew of 247 men. Many of the sailors were given shore leave where they attended parties, took moonlight walks on the Garrison, and watched a performance by the Spanish ballet dancer, Cyrene, in the Curtis Pavilion. Thursday was declared "Governor's Day" when Governor Elias Carr arrived to inspect the reserves and their vessels. Governor Carr and his family stayed at the home of Dr. and Mrs. Curtis on Moore Street while some of the Governor's party found accommodations at "Mrs. Greenbaum's boarding house next door," as Mrs. Curtis put it. Still others stayed at the Stuart House. The hostesses outdid themselves by providing delicious meals. The Southport band gave a serenade for the Governor and he "made a very neat little speech" followed by a torchlight parade. Town officials, the Curtis family, and visitors from Wilmington were invited to board the *Nantucket* with Governor Carr and his party. Here many champagne toasts were drunk and an enjoyable time was had by all, and as the Governor and his guests left the ship in the cutter boats, a 21-gun salute was fired. Later that evening a reception was held in the Pavilion with all the ships' officers in full dress. Mrs. Curtis wore a "black lace dress, trimmed with yellow, cut square in the neck." The "Governor's Day" festivities lasted until 1 a.m.

Friday held more excitement when the *Nantucket* began blowing her whistles "alarmingly." She had broken anchorage and was drifting toward the rocks. Fortunately, the nearby *Montgomery* gave assistance and soon all was quiet again. On Saturday, Dr. Curtis gave a stag party for all officers. Finally, on the following Tuesday, the ships left, and Mrs. Curtis confined to her diary that she was "feeling rather tired, with such continual excitement." Southport had indeed experienced a "gala week."

The United States Marine Hospital Service took control of all port quarantines from the states and appropriated $25,000 for a station building near Southport. On July 20, 1895, a contract for constructing the station in 90 days was awarded to Frank Baldwin of Washington, D.C.

Dr. J.M. Eager, a career officer in the U.S. Marine Hospital Service, was sent to Southport as quarantine officer. Dr. Curtis, who held the post for thirty years and worked diligently for adequate quarantine facilities, was replaced just as his goal was in sight. Naturally, he was deeply hurt and his family and friends were disturbed by this turn of events. Mrs. Curtis wrote in her diary of the hurt and despair they felt. Dr. Curtis had lost much of his money investing in the various railroad projects and now his income was to be "sadly reduced." Mrs. Curtis said that it gave them "great anxiety" because they were concerned about their sons' education as they were approaching college age.

The Curtises moved from Moore Street to what was called the Fremont Place. Mrs. Curtis did not mention why they moved nor the location of the new property. From other remarks it seems to have been waterfront property. When the Eagers arrived Mrs. Curtis recorded in her diary that they were "very agreeable people." Governor Elias Carr returned to visit Dr. Curtis and together they went coon hunting on Bald Head Island. After the diary entry telling of Governor Carr's visit, Mrs. Curtis' entries became sporadic, ceasing altogether in October 1896. One final statement was made about the railroad which she prayed for:

> There seemed to be a hitch in the railroad building down here (latest effort); it has stopped for want of money and gone into the receiver's hands; our railroad projects seem fated.

The building of the Quarantine Station began soon after the contract was awarded. It was located between the upper end of Battery Island and Price's Creek Lighthouse on the east side of the channel, one and a half miles from Southport. The station was to be built in the river on a pier 600 feet in length and was to consist of a hospital building, a disinfecting house with modern apparatus, attendants' quarters, and a kitchen. An artesian well was to furnish water for the station's use.

By July Mr. Baldwin had left the job unfinished. Another contractor was employed, and on September 22nd the newspaper announced that fumigation equipment and machinery was being installed and that the completion of all work was expected by

October 1st. However, it was not until May 1st of the next year that there is mention of the station in operation. The first ship to be quarantined at the new station was a British vessel *Cubana*. In June a Brazilian vessel, suspected to have yellow fever on board, was detained for ten days. Over the next six years, officers in charge of the station changed frequently, one of whom stayed less than eight months.

Federal Quarantine Station and Hospital.

For the next few years very little was mentioned about a railroad or a port, although a progressive attitude was still exhibited by the citizens. Streets were improved and renamed. What had originally been Discord Street became St. George Street and Potts Street became Atlantic Avenue. Sad to say, when this was done, Joshua Potts' name was erased from Southport. Boundary Street's name was renamed Caswell Street because Burrington and Clarendon Streets had been opened beyond what had once been the town boundary. At least two small new subdivisions opened on the west side. Town officials were concerned with "lighting the city" and a lamp committee was appointed. The Old Smithville Burying Ground was "repaired" and was declared in "thoroughly good condition." The aldermen hired "special police," but the town minutes do not indicate their purpose. They also ordered that "the Cedar Tree at the foot of Howe Street be protected by putting shells around its base." Alderman Williams had the work done for $1.40.

October 13 and 14, 1896, were great days in Southport—another chance for a big celebration. The newly commissioned U.S. Cruiser *Raleigh*, named for North Carolina's capital city, was brought safely across the bar by young pilot Edward Hall Adkins. Every house and building in town was gaily decorated with flags and bunting, and all harbor vessels were flying their flags. Governor Elias Carr and his staff along with several hundred Wilmingtonians arrived on Captain John W. Harper's steamer *Wilmington*. All of these people and Southport's dignitaries, boarded the ship for a special ceremony. A large silver punch bowl and ladle from North Carolina was presented to the *Raleigh* in appreciation for having been named for the City of Raleigh. Governor Carr and Samuel A'Court Ashe made pproriate addresses, and Captain Miller of the *Raleigh* accepted the gift with another speech. The 283 men aboard the ship gave three cheers followed by a banquet for all in attendance.

Compliments of **Wilmington & Southport Steamboat Company**

For an Enjoyable Day Spend it on the Historical Cape Fear

DAILY SCHEDULE:
Leave Wilmington at 9:30 a. m.
Leave Southport at 2:30 p. m.

SUNDAY SCHEDULE:
Leave Wilmington 9:30 a. m. and 2:30 p. m.
Leave Southport at 11:30 a. m. & 4:30 p. m.

STEAMER WILMINGTON OF WILMINGTON, N. C.   SPECIAL RATES FOR EXCURSIONS AND PARTIES

Captain John W. Harper was master of the steamer *Wilmington* which was the most famous of many ships that connected Smithville/Southport with the rest of the state and nation. The ship carried mail, produce, and passengers to and from Wilmington.

Samuel A'Court Ashe was a popular and beloved figure of the Cape Fear area. He had served as a captain in the Confederate Army during the Civil War and had founded the *News and Observer* in Raleigh. In addition, he edited the seven-volume *Biographical History of North Carolina* and wrote *History of North Carolina (1584-1783)*. A gifted orator and writer, he was referred to as "a loyal and devoted son of the Cape Fear."

The cruiser *Raleigh* saw service in Manila Bay during the brief war with Spain. In May of the year following the war, she made a triumphal return to the Cape Fear to deliver war trophies for the City of Raleigh. A delegation met the ship in Wilmington where another silver service was presented to the ship and the war trophies were received for the state.

As relationships with Spain deteriorated, the Cape Fear Pilots Association, sensing that war was inevitable, offered its services to the U.S. Government. Activity at Fort Caswell was feverish as needed improvements were rushed to completion. An electric light plan was installed in early 1898 so that work could be done around the clock. Submarine torpedoes were delivered and stored. Thirty-four cases of dynamite for Caswell were brought to Wilmington by rail and transported to the fort by the steamer *Wilmington*. A boiler and steam pump, a large dredge, and four mules were also sent in. Work was suspended on the river and harbor improvements as the laborers were sent to Fort Caswell to work on an additional gun emplacement. A thousand tons of quarry stone from Mount Airy were contracted for this new gun emplacement at the west end of the fort. The testing of the new heavy guns caused excitement and fear in Southport as windows rattled and pictures fell from walls. Soon, however, the citizens were assured that the Spanish were not invading.

Men from the U.S. Hospital Corps arrived to staff the fort's hospital. One man came from the Rock Island Arsenal, Illinois, to set up a commissary, and two experienced operators came to man the telegraph office. A handsome white horse for the fort surgeon's use was conveyed to Caswell by the steamer *Wilmington*. This steamer must have been kept very busy, constantly transporting men, supplies, and materials that had come to Wilmington by rail.

A telegraph line from the fort to Southport and then on to Wilmington was erected. Troops, arriving at Caswell on a regular basis for training, were transported to Cuba. Because the Cape Fear River below Wilmington was guarded by submarine mines, no vessel was allowed to pass through the channel from Battery Island to the sea buoy between sunset and sunrise. Patrol boats, authorized to stop vessels for identification, were stationed above and below the defenses to instruct ships on the passage through the mine fields.

As around-the-clock work continued at Caswell throughout the spring and summer; carpenters, masons, stone cutters, and other craftsmen found plenty of employment. The people and businesses in Southport were also caught up in all the activity. Application was made for a Sunday mail service to Southport. Military bands played for every occasion, and the music of the times included *The Girl I Left Behind Me*; *Dixie*; *Carolina*; and *Home, Sweet Home*. With a surge of patriotism, the rallying cry of *Remember the Maine* was heard often.

The war declared on April 20, 1898, ended on August 12 with the signing of a peace treaty. The United States emerged from the brief, fierce war as a new international power. Now the burning question in Southport was "What is to happen to Fort Caswell?" The answer, a few weeks later, was pleasing to the inhabitants. Fort Caswell would continue to operate and "rank with any fortification on the South Atlantic coast."

After buildup at the fort had ceased, the soldiers had more time to make trips to Wilmington. At times they created an uproar by frequenting the bars and becoming nuisances. On one occasion three of them had to be jailed by Wilmington police. In November the visiting Caswell troops caused so much trouble that their commanding officer requested Wilmington's police chief to arrest any soldier found without a pass. Although there are no extant records to confirm the theory, it is imagined that Southport often had the same kind of soldier problems.

For Southport, the last year of the nineteenth century began very quietly. In February, a bitter storm brought heavy snow. Reports say that the river between Southport and Bald Head was frozen for a distance of four miles.

At a special meeting of the Board of Aldermen in March, they decided the city could not afford to open a new cemetery, as had been proposed. They then left the matter for "the consideration of the incoming administration." The aldermen did, however, find enough money to pay for "marking and placing lamp posts on the streets." They also ordered a large quantity of crushed oyster shells for the streets. The mayor was instructed to purchase 25 galvanized tin buckets to be "marked and kept at the truck house." When a fire occurred in town:

> *The City Marshall shall have the fire truck and buckets taken as soon as possible to the scene of the fire, and that he shall take them back to the truck house as soon as the fire is over, and that all Ladders and Buckets be kept at the Truck House at all times when not in use for city purposes.*

A contract was signed in June for Southport's telephone line to be in use within 90 days. Also in June the aldermen addressed the problem of proper bathing attire by passing an ordinance declaring it:

*Unlawful for any person to bathe in the river and creeks within
the boundaries of the city in the day time without a suit covering their entire body from elbows to knees.*

Also, the aldermen declared a misdemeanor for driving horses
or mules attached to any vehicle on the Garrison. Another ordinance
forbade the cutting or whittling of any part of the "Garrison Bridge,"
and no lounging, loafing, or sitting on the "railings" of the bridge
would be tolerated. In the early fall, B.F. Greer was granted the
privilege of selling cider for one month at his butcher shop, and
J. Baker Fountain was granted the same privilege at Wescott's Store
"near the Garrison."

On the last two days of October all interest in mundane matters ceased as a hurricane bore down on the town. Marking the
same path that Hurricane Hazel followed in 1954, the storm moved
ashore to strike Southport and Fort Caswell. This storm caused great
damage and destruction, and it was reported to be "the worst storm
ever." A large steamer was wrecked off the coast, ten smaller vessels
were driven ashore, and the tug *Blanch* was beached at Southport.
Many oak trees were uprooted; the Stuart House and at least two
other waterfront dwellings were heavily damaged. At Caswell, the
damage was assessed at $50,000 with a million cubic yards of sand
washed away. The railroad washed out in several places, many small
buildings were destroyed, and 170 cords of wood were lost.

The debris cleared away, two new subdivisions, or "annexes"
were added to the town as the charter of the city had been amended to do. Mark Fargusson, a Chicago civil engineer living in
Southport, was engaged to make a new map showing the addi-
tions. Mr. Fargusson was to receive $30 for his services with half
paid from the 1899 tax levy and half from the 1900 levy.

In a study of Southport's architecture done by architectural
historian Carl Lounsbury in 1978, it is noted that of the buildings
depicted, twenty-two were built between 1800 and 1880 and twenty-
three between 1880 and 1890. In the next decade forty-two structures
were erected. Most of the new homes were built in the western
and northwestern areas that had opened for development. Clearly, the decade between 1890 and 1900 saw Southport's greatest surge
in the building industry until the era following World War II.

Prominent builders during Southport's heyday included the
Daniel brothers, Henry and Joseph; their relative by marriage,

A.J. Robbins; George Davis; and William T. Ottoway. Mr. Ottoway often broke from the traditional patterns followed by the others, and unless directed otherwise by customers, he included modern innovations of the Victorian age. By this time, house plans were more widely available, and more materials and better tools could be purchased in Southport and Wilmington. In 1894, A.E. Stevens completed a two and a half story house at the corner of Atlantic Avenue and Brown Street. Lounsbury noted its unique design:

> *The house in design, stylistic imagination and craftsmanship,*
> *is perhaps the highest achievement of architecture in Southport*
> *during its most active period, 1880-1920.*

Beautifully and carefully preserved, the house today is the home of Mr. and Mrs. A.F. Gavin.

During the 1890-1900 decade, new ordinances were enacted to deal with the problem of garbage and other offensive matter emptied into the river. These ordinances addressed streams inside the city, privies, vacant lots, animal pens, stables, and animals running at large.

A June 1898 ordinance states that it is unlawful to use profane or boisterous language in public places, and that concealed weapons are forbidden. Animals cannot run at large and bicycles must be equipped with "alarm bells" for day use and lighted lanterns at night. The city marshall must supervise ball games played in the streets or empty lots, and it is a misdemeanor for a person to mistreat any animal or to rob a bird's nest. Another misdemeanor was to deface the lamp posts, fences, shade trees, or buildings. Fines were imposed and enforced. Taxes were raised by a small amount and detailed accounts were given of collections and disbursements in the extant minutes of the Southport Board of Aldermen.

A New Century and
The Great War
1900-1919

As Southport entered the twentieth century, progress was still uppermost in the minds of her people. Change had become the American way of life, and was slowly arriving in Southport. Construction was somewhat sluggish, but forty-seven structures built in the first two decades of the new century are still standing today. Many were small cottages surrounded by picket fences (everything had picket fences, even the churches and Masonic Lodge) and small flower and bountiful vegetable gardens. These flower gardens contained plants found earlier in colonial gardens—spireas, snowdrops, periwinkles, Star-of-Bethlehem, daisies, oxalis, phlox, gardenias, and roses. One of the climbing roses was locally called a "cemetery rose." Most housewives raised chickens, not only for their eggs, but to have chicken on the table every Sunday. Housecleaning and cooking were done each Saturday; Sunday was a day of rest and church-going.

Southport citizens enjoyed making their own musical and dramatic presentations. Plays and skits were presented at the Pavilion or the Academy. Bands flourished and pianos were in most homes where family and friends gathered to sing songs as "In the Shade of the Old Apple Tree," "Sweet Adeline," and "Let Me Call you Sweetheart." Sheet music, brought by steamer from Wilmington, was easily available. Self-player pianos were in vogue, and a few were found in Southport homes. Some families were the proud possessors of phonographs which furnished music for dancing.

Once again citizens and town officials began promoting a railroad. In May and June of 1900, they organized a Chamber of Commerce. Officers were president, Marshall C. Guthrie; vice president, Dr. Walter G. Curtis; secretary, W. H. Pyke; and, treasurer,

Richard Dosher. The Mayor and Board of Aldermen granted rights-of-way on two tracts of land to the newly chartered Southport, Wilmington, and Western Railroad Company. These two tracts were located on Moore Street from Bonnet's Creek to Rhett Street, and from the east side of Kingsley Street down Bay Street to the western line of Boundary Street. (Sometimes they still used the old names for the recently re-named streets.)

The U.S. Revenue Cutter *Algonquin,* stationed at Southport for the summer, created a "great demand" for summer housing. While the railroad and port development were visions, tourism flourished, as it had from the town's earliest days.

The Wilmington and Southport Telegraph Company improved its lines between towns. The next year, Dr. E.G. Goodman of Town Creek erected a telephone line from Jacques Creek to the Brunswick River bridge. In the early fall of 1901, the Columbus Telephone Company built a line from Southport to Wilmington. On October 16, 1901, Southport's telephone system was established with twenty-two phones. The central office was located at the residence of William St. George on West Moore Street. His two daughters, Margaret and Eva, managed this downtown office. In November, Southport and Wilmington were connected, but calls to Wilmington could only be made from pay booths with three-minute calls costing fifteen cents.

The town seemed famous for big celebrations such as the one on Labor Day, 1901. The festivities lasted from 10 a.m. until 11 p.m. and included a parade, band music, games, races, and the usual orations. The Second Regiment Band of Wilmington gave an open-air concert in Franklin Square which was gaily illuminated by colorful Japanese lanterns.

In October, the U.S. Weather Bureau erected a 50-foot steel tower, with a 25-foot staff, on the Garrison lawn. Mr. Enoch B. Stevens was "in charge." His daughter, Jessie Margaret (later Mrs. C. Ed Taylor) became the volunteer weather observer, receiving reports and displaying appropriate flags on the tower. Until her death in 1961 at the age of 82, Mrs. Taylor served in this capacity. In 1955 she was honored in Washington, D.C. as the oldest female weather observer in the United States. In presenting the Meritorious Service Award and the 50-year Service Medal to this faithful volunteer, Weather Bureau officials stated:

*Mrs. Taylor's prompt action in displaying signal flags and lights
on the weather tower (prior to Hurricane Hazel) gave warning
of approaching hurricanes to both coastwise shipping and people living in the area and undoubtedly saved hundreds of lives.*

A bronze marker, erected by officers of the Sunny Point Army Terminal, on the Garrison lawn commemorates Jesse Taylor's service.

In January 1902, the Cape Fear Pilots Association mourned the
loss of James Harmon Chadbourn, Chairman of the Board of Commissioners of Navigation and Pilotage for twenty-two years. During his tenure he was successful in getting the N.C. General
Assembly to enact legislation providing income for destitute widows
and children of deceased pilots.

The hope for a railroad was ever present as evidenced by the
organization of the Southport Land Company in March. The purpose of this company, organized by W.H. Pyke of Southport, R.W.
Hicks of Wilmington, and three Philadelphia businessmen, was to
develop a coaling station in Southport. For several years Mr. Pyke
had been buying land on the outskirts of town and in partnership
with J.A. Pullan and William Weeks had opened several small
subdivisions.

In June 1902, the residents of Southport were saddened when
the last cannon was taken from Fort Johnston by the U.S. Corps
of Engineers and transported by steamer to Savannah, Georgia or
Charleston, S.C. The cannon was a 10-inch Columbiad which had
been placed at the fort in 1862. The following week, C. Ed Taylor,
editor of the *Southport Standard*, wrote a front-page article lament-
ing the cannon's removal:

*Perhaps there is nothing in the shape of an old landmark more
dear to the people of Southport and those who claim the town
as their old home than the old Civil War relic that has stood
a modest guard for nearly a half century on the site of old Fort
Johnston . . . The cannon carries with it the associations of
two generations.*

This disappointment was soon put aside as citizens prepared
for a busy tourist season. Commenting on this in February 1903,
the newspaper stated:

*With good lights on our streets, a deep well of pure water, our
streets and sidewalks repaired and improved, to which we may*

add a cool and refreshing sea breeze, fresh from the Atlantic Ocean at all times, Southport can throw open her doors of welcome to the visitors next summer.

Visitors and summer residents were heartily welcomed as they arrived in town. They brought new life and vigor just as they had each summer since the days of old Smithville.

The local newspaper continued to report on building activity. A new Presbyterian Church was erected on a slope of land on Caswell Street which was called "Presbyterian Hill." Previously church officials turned down a building site in Franklin Square near the Baptist and Methodist Churches. "Presbyterian Hill" was a favorite place for roller skating and bicycle riding as youth gathered there after school, on weekends, and on summer days. The new white-framed church's interior paneling was like that of the other three churches in town.

Brunswick County Commissioners voted to improve the dilapidated courthouse and jail. Bids were accepted for a new jail to be erected at the corner of Nash and Rhett Streets on a parcel of land purchased from Miss Kate Stuart. No one brought up the controversial subject of moving the county seat, and the work proceeded. Contractor A.J. Robbins received the contract for the jail, and the construction was supervised by Henry Daniel. Completed in 1904, the building housed prisoners until 1971 when it was replaced by a one-story jail facing Rhett Street just to the rear of the 1904 structure. The "Old Jail" became an office for the Brunswick County Sheriff's Department. When the new government complex was completed and the county seat moved to Bolivia in 1978, title to the land and buildings passed to the City of Southport. The "Old Jail" was leased to the Southport Historical Society as its headquarters. The Historical Society established the "Benjamin Smith Memorial Garden" around the building. In addition, the Rhett Street jail was leased to the local chapter of Disabled American Veterans.

Aware of the need for improved educational opportunities, town leaders met in April 1903 to discuss changing the local school system into a public, graded school. By a unanimous decision, current city appropriations were designated for construction of a new school building. On October 13 an educational rally raised $125 toward the project, and a committee was appointed to oversee arrangements for the school. In August 1904, the contract was awarded to Moses A. McKeithan for $2,800.00 which was $60 lower than his fellow bidder, A.J. Robbins. The funds were hard to raise but the Junior Order of United American Mechanics, a patron of education, worked hard through completion of the project. The new building, located on Dry Street in Franklin Square, was built on lots originally reserved by the town's founders for educational, religious and fraternal purposes. On Thanksgiving Day 1904, the whole town witnessed the laying of the cornerstone supervised by the Junior Order. The building was completed quickly and the graded school opened. When the school outgrew the building in 1918, two one-story wings were added for extra classrooms. This building was used as a school until after 1930.

As part of the county's school consolidation program in the late 1920s, a large, brick school was erected on the corner of Nash and Dry Streets. Soon all Smithville district students were housed in the brick building located where today's U.S. Post Office sits. The old frame school was then converted into Southport's City Hall. When the county seat moved to Bolivia, deed restrictions called for the courthouse and its land to revert to the City of Southport. When town hall moved into the old courthouse, the former school-city hall building became headquarters for a Southport art group. This building is now known as Franklin Square Art Gallery.

Construction was booming across the bay at Fort Caswell. Carpenters, masons, and other craftsmen were busy as additional housing was completed for a captain and several non-commissioned officers. A hospital, guardhouse, and jail were constructed. The new hospital was proclaimed ''one of the best the government has ever built.'' Officers and non-commissioned officers were allowed to have families with them at the fort, and several Southport women who married soldiers were among those living on the reservation.

Much travel took place back and forth across the bay on government-owned steamers and commercial steamers owned by Captain John W. Harper and others. C. Ed Taylor, a Town Creek resident who moved to Southport and was newspaper editor, received his law license in September 1904. He set up his practice in Southport and was scheduled to plead his first case in the Brunswick County court that same month. By the following year, Mr. Taylor was representing Brunswick County in the State Legislature. As his practice rapidly grew, he developed a special expertise in real estate law. In 1939, a young Robeson County lawyer, E.J. Prevatte, became a partner, with their office located in the E.B. Stevens Building on Moore Street. Mr. Taylor continued to practice law in Southport until his death in 1944.

In June 1909, Mr. Taylor married Jessie Margaret Stevens. After a northern honeymoon, they lived in Southport where they supported many worthwhile causes, both financially and with volunteer service, throughout their lives. Mrs. Taylor, along with several other town matrons, organized the Southport Civic Club, forerunner of today's Southport Woman's Club. This club has always played an active part in every notable civic project of Southport. The Taylor's daughter, Margaret (now Mrs. James M. Harper, Jr.), continues actively in the club organized by her mother. The Taylor legacy of service to the community is still carried on by its family members.

The old Fort Johnston site remained important to Southport's people. Various attempts were made by the citizens to improve the Garrison for use as a park. The structures remaining, including the officers quarters and the bakehouse, needed repairs. In February 1906, a petition was circulated asking Senator Furnifold Simmons to seek an appropriation from Congress. The purpose of this appropriation was to improve the colonial site and to assure that it not be used for "utility purposes." The bill, when finally introduced in February 1908, also provided for the construction of a retaining wall along the river. There is no evidence that such a wall was ever built.

In the spring of 1906, machinery arrived for the new sawmill on Walden (Waldron) Creek. Soon in operation, the mill supplied lumber for another flurry of construction in Southport and at Fort Caswell. Also, Seaboard Air Lines Railroad purchased land, previously owned by the Southern and Western Railroad, near Bonnet's Creek. This railroad proposed entering Southport from the east.

The usual Fourth of July celebration was held with boat races and fireworks. This year a new dimension was added as Fort Caswell was open for inspection. Steamers took visitors across the bay for a tour of the military base.

In mid-September a destructive tropical storm approached the coast from the east-southeast and moved inland south of Myrtle Beach, S.C. where considerable damage was done to marine vessels. Several disabled vessels were towed to the Southport harbor and then to Wilmington for repairs. During the storm, the lightship went adrift, but was rescued by the U.S. buoy tender *Wisteria*. "The Rocks," the engineering feat which had closed New Inlet twenty years before, suffered over $100,000 in damages. Recollections say that one ton stone blocks were tossed fifty feet by the terrific force of the wind. Following this storm, Captain John W. Harper's steamer *Wilmington* made a special excursion from Wilmington to Southport for her 400 passengers to see wrecked schooners and damages at "The Rocks."

In October, 36 Southport business and professional people, including five women, and two men from Wilmington, purchased stock in the Brunswick Transportation Company. Evidently, these business people had given up hope for a railroad in Southport, because the purpose of the new company was to place a freight and passenger steamer on the Cape Fear to ply between Southport and Wilmington. The New York steamers *Mary* and *Atlantic* were purchased along with property in Wilmington at Dock and Water Streets. Buildings and wharves at this location were to be remodeled for use. The following January, Captain Harper added the 300-passenger steamer *Madeleine* to his fleet. The *Madeleine* made stops at Carolina Beach, Southport, Fort Caswell and Wilmington. Indications were that river traffic was heavy.

Also in January, the Wilmington, Brunswick, and Southern, another railroad company was chartered. The capital stock was $200,000 and the principal incorporators were Wilmington citizens. Although the company would eventually run a railroad line into Southport, most townspeople considered this railroad line just another pipedream or false promise. Instead of being excited about another railroad company, they busied themselves by keeping their streets clean, properly lighting the street lamps, and enforcing sanitation ordinances. Citizens struggled to pay their city taxes at a tax rate of thirty cents per hundred dollar valuation. The poll tax was used for school purposes. The "Kilston light," located at the intersection of Moore and Potts Streets, was moved to the intersection of Nash and Howe Streets, nearer the town center where there was increased night traffic. The number of street lamps is unknown, but pictures show one located at the corner of Nash and Howe Streets.

In March, the river pilots had a reason to celebrate with rejoicing and bonfires. News came from Raleigh stating that the General

Assembly had enacted legislation establishing new rules and regulations governing pilotage over the Cape Fear bar. A month later, Governor Robert B. Glenn, under the current act, appointed a new Board of Navigation and Pilotage to four-year terms. This Board was given authority to enforce rules and regulations provided in the act and to issue commissions to pilots. Two Southport men, Richard Dosher and M.C. Guthrie, were appointed to the Board. Three Wilmington members included Captain John W. Harper who maintained a second residence in Southport while operating his many steamers between the towns. M.C. Guthrie was elected mayor of Southport. The river continued to be the focus of attention in town.

In August, Wilmington, Brunswick, and Southern drove the first spike near Navassa for its railroad. There was little notice taken of this in Southport. The town officials were much more concerned about the gates in the fence surrounding the town that were being carelessly left open. Mayor Guthrie ordered a ten-dollar fine to be charged to:

> *Any person who shall unlock, unlatch, unfasten, open or partially open any gate in the public fence inclosing the city, and leave same unhooked, unlatched, unfastened, open or partially opened.*

In February 1908, the First Baptist Church, the first black Baptist church in Southport, was established. The Rev. Castilla Goodman was the pastor, serving his congregation for 37 years. The membership steadily increased and by the church anniversary in September 1976 had reached more than a hundred members. For this anniversary, 91-year-old member Mrs. Maggie Behivelle supplied much information to the church historian for a written history. Today ,the church at 907 North Lord Street is still progressing with organizations in all age-levels. Significant anniversaries were also observed in 1983 and 1988.

Roads near Southport were inadequate, and most travel remained by water. However, mail from Lockwood Folly and other areas of Brunswick County came to the county seat over township roads. Some farm products were also brought into Southport via horse and wagon.

Work began on a new shell road toward Lockwood Folly in the fall of 1908 when the Smithville township voted a $12,000 bond issue for the road. Contractor A.J. Robbins hired nearly 100 men for the road's construction.

The recently failed Bank of Southport was taken over by Thomas E. and W.B. Cooper of Wilmington and became a "safe and progressive institution." Boat building was flourishing in Southport and a special racing model with an engine capable of doing 20 miles-per-hour was built for newspaper editor Howard C. Curtis and his brother, Professor Nathaniel Courtland Curtis.

In May, the Southport and Little River Telephone Company was chartered for operation, thus widening the scope of communications for the town. By June, Southern Bell purchased the Southport to Wilmington line. Also in June, the first mail was opened at the new post office building on East Moore Street; J.J. Loughlin erected a new store at the corner of Moore and Howe Streets; and, at least five homes were under construction.

The town obtained a new charter from the state, giving the Board of Aldermen authority to provide for water, sewer, electricity, curbing, and street paving. Things were progressing! Howard C. Curtis, editor of the *Southport Herald*, felt impelled to plead that the town not allow commercial development to destroy the natural beauty and charm of the town. He wrote:

> *When any well informed observer notices a disposition on the part of municipal authorities to preserve and safeguard natural decorative features such as trees and to perpetuate historical landmarks unaltered and to add various improvements that will tend to make a town more attractive, he realizes that town is destined always to have a unique individuality and charm above other towns. More than that, this characteristic often includes and carries with it a genuine commercial asset. The people who live in such a town are proud of it and prefer to spend their lives there, and visitors always come back. Many a man would not hesitate to sacrifice a century-old tree because it partially concealed his view of a railroad train. We can recall any number of towns near home where the streets have been entirely denuded of trees in the first instance with the idea that the result enhanced the metropolitan aspect of the embryo city . . . Southport already a naturally beautiful little city could be made more so but it is hoped that when the inevitable growth to a larger and greater municipality comes that this natural beauty will not be sacrificed to commercialism.*

On August 9, 1909, the town was deeply saddened by the death of their beloved doctor, friend, and civic leader, Walter Gilman Curtis. Shortly before his death he wrote a small volume entitled *Reminiscences of Wilmington and Smithville-Southport, 1848-1900.* The booklet, published by his son, Howard (editor of the Southport newspaper), and Mrs. Curtis' diary have helped immeasurably in piecing together the Southport story of that period.

In August 1910, the first automobile came to town. Bill Reaves in his *Chronology* of Southport recalls:

> *Mr. and Mrs. W.H. Stone of Little River, S.C. were in Southport recently. They were accompanied by Mr. Henry Bridgers, of Bladenboro, who brought them overland in his automobile, which was the first machine to reach Southport.*

An event of more immediate importance took place in 1911 when the Southport Building and Loan Association was chartered. The organizational meeting was held in the Moore Street office of attorneys E.H. Cranmer and Robert W. Davis. Officers elected were: M.C. Guthrie, president; S.B. Northrop, vice president; and Dr. D.I. Watson, secretary-treasurer and managing officer. Dr. Watson, a physician, pharmacist, and astute business man, recognized the need for a lending institution that encouraged thrift and financed home construction for Southport citizens. A plan was devised for potential borrowers to buy shares in the association for as little as 25 cents a share per week.

Dr. Watson kept the new organization's records in a corner of his drugstore, Watson's Pharmacy. (Today this building houses a restaurant called The Pharmacy.) Later Southport Building and Loan Association moved into its office across the street from Watson's Pharmacy in a 1920s building erected for attorney E.H. Smith. Dr. Watson served as managing officer for the Southport Building and Loan Association until his retirement in 1933 when James E. Carr became secretary-treasurer. Later the association moved to larger quarters on Moore Street, and eventually to its present location at the corner of Howe and Moore Streets. As the institution experienced steady growth, the name was changed to Southport Savings & Loan Association and finally to Security Savings and Loan Association. The Association has several branch offices in Brunswick County and has made it possible for the American dream of home ownership to come true for thousands of people during its eighty years of existence.

The year 1911 also saw a flurry of business and construction activity from several sectors. A Mrs. Atwood of Southport was granted a franchise by the city to operate an electric power plant when she proposed to spend $15,000 to establish the business. H.W. Hood erected a two-story brick building on the corner of Moore and Davis Streets for his expanding dry goods business. (Today this building houses the Dosher Memorial Flea Market.)

The *Southport News*, the first county newspaper to be operated by women, began publication in July. Editors Emma C. Atwood and Kate E. Griswold announced that the newspaper would "work for legislation to better the cause of women; to make it a better world for women."

A contract was awarded to A.J. Robbins to construct a bank building on Moore Street, adjoining Watson's Pharmacy. Directors for the Bank of Brunswick were named from several areas of the county-Southport, Shallotte, Town Creek, and Waccamaw. About this time, a floating fish factory, capable of producing 10,000 barrels of fish per day, arrived to begin operations in Southport.

Several new residences were built and the *Southern Pines Tourist* excitedly predicted that Southport's harbor would soon be the "nearest harbor of highest rank to the Panama Canal" which was then under construction. The paper also said that "Southport's more enthusiastic boomers feel sure that Southport will some day practically wipe Wilmington off the map" as the state's chief port.

"Southport Gloriously Celebrating Today" proclaimed headlines in the Wilmington *Evening Dispatch* of November 23, 1911. After many years of dreaming, dashed hopes, and speculation, a railroad line into Southport became a reality. The paper carried pictures of Governor William Walton Kitchin, U.S. Senator Furnifold Simmons, Congressman H.L. Godwin and Z.W. Whitehead, President of Wilmington, Brunswick and Southern Railroad Company, who were present at the celebration.

> *With colors streaming and banners and bunting fore, aft and amidships the first passenger train of the Wilmington, Brunswick and Southern Railroad left from the union depot this morning in the midst of joyous excitement. The five coaches of the train were crowded with passengers who were eager to take part in the grand celebration of the opening of the road*

at Southport today. The weather was perfect and indications pointed to a day ideal for the occasion . . . On the front coach were the former Brunswick Boys - men who were former residents of Southport, but who later moved to this city, very appropriately returned for a visit to the home town on the momentous occasion of the day in a body, riding in a chartered car. The car was crowded with the ''boys'', each of whom was jolly as a lark. They solemnly affirm, that since they have grouped themselves that they have discovered themselves to be the handsomest bunch of men they ever saw. Fully 100 of the former sons of Southport took advantage of the opportunity to attend the celebration on the special car . . . Dr. Russell Bellamy was the first to purchase a ticket over the new road.

Railroad station of the WB&S Railroad, 1911. Faced Moore Street, near Old Smithville Burying Ground.

Many other visitors attended the celebration, arriving from the city on the steamer *Wilmington*. The train trip took two hours and 36 minutes; the two modes of transportation arrived in Southport at the same time. Greeting the visitors were Fort Caswell's officers, Southport's Chamber of Commerce representatives, and many town citizens. Anchored in the harbor were two torpedo boats and the U.S. Revenue Cutter *Seminole*. The celebrants moved from the train station to ''the Oak Grove'' (Franklin Square) for the speeches. Attorney Robert W. Davis gave the welcome address which was

91

lengthily responded to by Major Joseph D. Smith of Wilmington. Congressman Godwin, Wilmington attorney J.O. Carr, and President Whitehead made short speeches. However, Senator Simmons spoke for over an hour in his "noted eloquent style." A gold cane, purchased by public subscription, was presented by C. Ed Taylor to the railroad president.

It is sadly noted that E.B. Stevens, early supporter of a Southport (Smithville) railroad, was not mentioned during the festivities even though he was still living. Dr. W.G. Curtis, another ardent supporter of a town railroad, had died just two years before. His name was mentioned briefly by one of the speakers.

The city entertained visitors at a picnic dinner and barbecue in the square after the speeches were complete. Following the picnic, a motor boat race was viewed from the Garrison lawn. Back at "the Grove," a 100-yard dash state competition was held, and a bayonet drill by Fort Caswell soldiers was performed. While the Fort Caswell band played throughout the day, several other games and races were held. The steamer *General G.W. Getty* made regular trips to and from Fort Caswell during the afternoon for the accommodation of visitors.

In the early evening a large banquet was held for the dignitaries at the U.S. Quarantine Station about a mile and a half from Southport. The banquet was hosted by Dr. Bryan who had succeeded Dr. Curtis as quarantine officer. That occasion called for toasts and more speeches. The newspaper reported on the event:

> The large hospital was used as a dining room and was very clearly decorated. The walls were bordered with palms from Bald Head. The centerpiece of the ceiling decoration was a striking effect, gained by draping the North Carolina flag with the national colors. The decorations were done by Sergeant E.E. Wilson, of the 31st C.A.C. Fort Caswell.
>
> E.H. Cranmer, Esq., of the Southport Chamber of Commerce, presided as toastmaster at the banquet and the following responded to toasts: J.O. Carr, Esq., "The Old North State," which was drunk standing; Mayor Joseph D. Smith, "Wilmington and Southport, Twin Cities;" Hon. John D. Bellamy, "Southport, the City South of Cape Hatteras;" Col. C.A. Bennett, commanding Fort Caswell, "Relation Between Coast Artillery and Commerce;" Capt. John G. Berry of the Seminole,

92

> *"Commerce and the Revenue Cutter Service;" Lieut. S.B.*
> *Smith, commanding the MacDonnough and DeLong,*
> *"Southport as a Coaling Station."*
>
> *This closed the speeches, and three cheers were given for Dr.*
> *Bryan, the quarantine officer, who had made the entertainment*
> *of the guests possible by his hospitality.*

Although no women had been included in the official celebration, the feisty Kate Stuart, then 79 years old, rode a hand car into town on the morning of the celebration and wrote a poem for the occasion which was published in the *Southport Herald* and the *Wilmington Dispatch*:

> *On old Rhett Street each one you meet*
> *Just shakes hands all around,*
> *For don't you see, they say with glee,*
> *The railroad's come to town.*
>
> *From far Supply to Calabash,*
> *See how they cover ground,*
> *They've come to help us celebrate,*
> *The railroad's come to town.*
>
> *Good farmer Pyke, just from the "Pole",*
> *Who often used to frown,*
> *Now wears a vast substantial smile,*
> *The railroad's come to town.*
>
> *Bring out your flags, let's all hurrah!*
> *And do the thing up brown,*
> *It's been coming forty years,*
> *By Jinks, its got to town!*

Each afternoon at five o'clock, the train from Wilmington reached the Southport depot on Rhett Street bringing passengers and freight. For the townspeople this was an interesting part of their day; everyone dressed up to meet the train, especially on Sundays. The freight handlers were there with their hand carts and horse-drawn vehicles to pick up freight and deliver it to area businesses.

Annie May Woodside, whose grandmother ran the Clemmons House near the station, was a student at State Normal College (now UNC at Greensboro). She was delighted to leave Southport by train, change to another in Wilmington, and then go on to Greensboro. For a school project she wrote a short history of the town and closed it with words that summed up the feelings of the people of Southport about their railroad:

> *The dream of many years has been realized, but it remains to be seen how the town will use her opportunities. Surely great development will come with the opening of the Panama Canal.*

The next spring the town experienced a building boom with at least twenty-five buildings under contract or construction. Mayor Price Furpless said the city was "a veritable hot bed of building activity," and it was difficult to get building materials to meet demand. He declared the streets were thronged with "strangers who have come to Southport to investigate conditions and invest in land in and around town."

The Southport Civic Club, under the leadership of Jessie Stevens Taylor, opened a public library in a wing of the Officers Quarters at old Fort Johnston. Carrie Dosher became first librarian, and on August 29, 1912, Gertrude Loughlin, the daughter of Mr. and Mrs. J.J. Loughlin, checked out the first book, *Rebecca of Sunnybrook Farm*. The club raised money for their new project by holding "Progressive Teas" hosted by Mesdames D.O. Daniel, J.W. Thompson, R.W. Davis, P.J. Lumley, Will Davis, B.F. Stiffler, and Miss Carrie Dosher. Many town citizens donated books from their personal libraries, and soon there was a collection of over five hundred volumes.

The library was club supported for many years until the city began making small contributions toward the librarian's salary. Today the library has a collection of over 60,000 volumes, has nine employees, and is part of the Brunswick County Library system with three branches and another in the planning stage. Throughout the years the Southport Woman's Club has continued to give support to the library in all its stages of growth.

Early in 1913 a new well was sunk in "the Grove." This 146-foot deep well and pump replaced the 100-foot well drilled in 1902 and had a concrete drinking basin for draft animals. Dry Street was open through Franklin Square and horse drawn-vehicles hauling freight, produce, and trash made frequent stops at the basin. Citizens who lived near the well carried much of their drinking water from the town pump to their homes until the late 1920s. The water was unusually cool with a delightful taste and when tested in February of 1913 it was termed the "purest water ever analyzed by United States laboratories."

That same month, the Southport Light and Power Company was chartered, and the town enjoyed electric street lights for the first time. The original light was located on Moore Street with a promise that all streets would be well-lighted soon. In many towns throughout the nation electricity was furnished from dusk to midnight and apparently Southport was no exception. The street lights were turned on for short periods several nights during the first week, but Mr. Stiffler, the electrician and manager, promised that soon there would be continuous service "with no attention to whether the moon shines or not."

Southport continued to prosper. The Southport Ice Manufacturing Company, the Cape Fear Laundry and Manufacturing Company, and the Carolina Coast Products were newly organized businesses in town. Captain John W. Harper added another steamer to his fleet to ply between Wilmington, Southport, and Fort Caswell. The two existing banks were merged under the name of the Bank of Southport. The guest book at the Stuart House showed registrations from nearly every state in the Union as the boardinghouse experienced its best season ever.

Although the town seemed to be booming, Independence Day was celebrated quietly in 1913 with only a boat race, some family picnics, and a baseball game between the Southport and the Fort Caswell teams.

The Southport Civic Club raised money for additional benches on the Garrison lawn and damaged ones were replaced. The Garrison and "the Grove" (sometimes called Oak Grove) were favorite spots for any public gatherings, courting couples, or fundraising activities. Often the women's organizations held "ice cream suppers" and cakewalks at the Garrison to raise money for projects.

The 1913 fall session at the Southport High school opened with an enrollment of 217, an increase of 35 students from the previous year. A tenth grade had been added in 1912 and the faculty consisted of a principal and three teachers. M.C. Guthrie, County Superintendent of Education, announced that compulsory education would be enforced and an attendance officer was appointed. Mr. Guthrie presented the school with a world globe, atlas, and dictionary.

The globe and map were soon needed as the assassination of

Archduke Francis Ferdinand on June 28, 1914, in Sarajevo focused world attention on European troubles. When Germany declared war on Russia on August 2nd there was apprehension in Southport that the United States would be drawn into the developing conflict. Knowing the strength of Fort Caswell, across the bay, seemed to soothe some of the apprehension. However, a few days later, fears arose again when a German ship loaded with coffee came into the Southport harbor to avoid capture at sea. Another German ship and two British ships were already at anchor awaiting orders. However, the four ships soon departed without incident.

After being under construction for ten years, the Panama Canal opened to shipping in 1914 during President Woodrow Wilson's first term in office. The completion of the canal influenced the use of Southport's small coaling station, and war news from Europe made its use even more important.

Menhaden fishing fleet.

By this time, menhaden fishing was a big industry for Southport with two factories on the river above the town. Most of the menhaden were processed for the oil used in the manufacture of paints, linoleum, tanning solutions, soaps, and waterproof fabrics. The dried scrap was used for fertilizer and for feed for cattle, poultry, and swine. The fish not used for either purpose were sent to other coastal towns to be used as bluefish bait. J.W. Dey of New Jersey, a pioneer in the menhaden industry, moved to Southport and, with his brother, established the Southport Fish Scrap and Oil Company.

96

This factory was located on the Elizabeth River (now the Intracoastal Waterway). Later, another company, the Brunswick Navigation Company, built a plant nearby.

A large number of menhaden boats operated out of the Southport harbor offering employment to many men on boats and in factories. Purse seines, large container-type nets hung between surface floats with weights along the base, were used to catch the fish. In making a haul, two small boats (called purse boats) dropped nets in a circle and after enclosing a school of fish, a heavy weight was attached to the purse line and dropped overboard. The purse line was then hauled in, causing the bottom of the net to close like a drawstring purse. The large boat then came alongside and a dip net was used to scoop the fish from the purse net into the ship's hold. This was back-breaking, boring work, and the men sang as they worked to relieve the monotony. The men on the purse boats worked their nets in unison to the rhythm of their sea chanteys, made up as they worked. These chanteys, believed to have originated in North Carolina, became world famous and are the subject of many books and articles. Currently recordings are being sold, and one group of menhaden fishermen makes singing appearances at festivals, radio programs, and on television. Today, motors, winches, and hoses perform the work once done by human muscles, and their sounds replace the chanteys.

Menhaden fishermen pulling in the purse nets.

When menhaden boats returned in late afternoon with their day's catch, the vessels' whistles sounded to tell the townspeople the size of the catch. The first three toots of the whistle meant

97

"we're coming in with fish." After that, each toot represented 100,000 fish, as measured in metal containers. When the first three whistle sounds came, all activity ceased until other toots were counted. One preacher said he once had to suspend a prayer meeting while the congregation counted.

At the factory, the fish were processed by cooking them in huge vats. A strong, foul odor could be smelled for several miles, but none of the Southport citizens complained. Their answer to complaining visitors was—"That's Southport money you smell."

Dorothy Bell Kauffman (1915-1963), a beloved Southport woman, wrote a poem that expressed the general feeling:

THE SMELL OF SOUTHPORT MONEY

Don't you dare turn up your noses
When you come to Southport town,
If the wind's from a direction
That'll bring the fish-stink down—
For you don't belong among us
If you sniff and snort and sneeze
When the smell of Southport money
Comes driftin' down the breeze!

For the oil from the menhaden
Is our biggest "money crap"—
And the "fertilize" that's made from
Dryin' out the pogy scrap.
So don't get out your kerchief
When they're tryin' out the oil—
You can smell that Southport money
When the kettles start to boil!

When the pogies are a-runnin'
We earn butter for our bread;
If the season is a bad one—
We may eat it plain instead.
But our boys can buy new brogans
And our women have new hats
When the smell of Southport money
Comes creepin' cross the flats!

(from *The Inheritance of My Fathers*)

98

In the midst of progress, devastation struck. On February 15, 1915, a fire of unknown origin blazed through the business district and destroyed many buildings, while scorching the trees and other buildings. Some of the city record books and those of the electric company were also burned. Soldiers from Fort Caswell saw the blaze and came quickly across the bay to help fight the fire. By late March some businesses were back in operation and others followed quickly.

That same month, another event created much local excitement. A "mysterious airship" was seen near Southport. "It traveled very quickly and was about 500 feet in the air." The only "flying machine" known to be in the lower Cape Fear area was owned by Price Aviation Company. The sighted machine did not belong to Price and its origin was never determined. Nothing more was heard of it but, with the nation moving closer and closer to war, some citizens were fearful of the unknown airship.

Building activity at Fort Caswell intensified causing an impact on the local economy. Lumber for the fort was supplied by Brunswick County businesses, such as the E. Sellers Lumber Company of Supply and others in Bolivia. Men from many areas of the county cut and furnished wood for heating, cooking, and other uses at Caswell. Due to inadequate roads, lumber and wood were floated down the Elizabeth River or brought to Southport and taken across the bay on barges or steamers. The entrance to the fort was on the river side where steamers, which made several runs daily across the bay and from Wilmington, tied up.

February 12, 1915, was an important day for Southport; on that date construction began on a brick building to house the new "splendid" theater promised ten months earlier. Mayor Price Furpless had sold an old store building located on Howe Street between Nash and Moore, and the new owner moved it away. Mr. Furpless and C.E. Gause were already operating a movie theater, the Amuzu (pronounced amuse you), next door with "the latest improved Edison machine to show the latest moving pictures." The business had grown and expansion was necessary for "moving pictures, theatrical troupes, and other amusements." According to research by Carl Lounsbury, author of *The Architecture of Southport*, the brick building was not ready for occupancy until 1918. This delay was probably due to the scarcity of building materials and labor as most workmen in the area were employed in the massive buildup at Fort Caswell. This theater, the second Amuzu, was operated for over sixty years by the Furpless family and brought hours of happiness to many Brunswick County citizens.

Southport citizens were disturbed when Brunswick County's representative in the General Assembly introduced a bill calling for the move of the county seat from Southport to Bolivia. Although the issue had been discussed several times in the past, nothing had come of it. This time the people of Southport were incensed, and there was strong talk of creating a new county to encompass of Smithville Township. This measure would make it difficult for the remainder of the county to operate because a quarter of all county taxes was paid by Smithville. Once again the matter was squelched for a few years.

After the county seat furor died, it was back to business for the town. A sawmill went into operation nearby to help supply the ever increasing demand for the building industry. Less than 25% of Southport's houses were wired for electricity and the city began a house-wiring campaign. Payment for the wiring could be made on easy terms, but the payments were the responsibility of the tenants not the owners. The sand-clay road through the business district was widened to twelve feet and the road from Southport to Supply was improved. Perhaps this was done to pacify those who had been insistent on moving the county seat because of the difficultly in reaching Southport. Construction started on a road along the Cape Fear River from Southport to Wilmington which became known locally as the "River Road" or the Shell Road."

Operations of the water system was turned over to the City government. The water tank at the corner of Brown and Howe Streets was filled with 600,000 gallons of water, and all fire hydrants were tested. On January 21, 1916, a volunteer fire department was formally organized as officers were elected, a constitution and by-laws were adopted, and some necessary equipment was purchased. Soon there was a fire alarm bell and an engine house with hoses and reels located in Franklin Square at the same location as today's fire department.

The next month Southeastern Underwriters Association of Atlanta issued a special and detailed report on the town for insurance purposes. The report gave a population estimate of between 1,700 and 1,800, and a tax valuation of $700,000. The tax rate was $1.25. The report stated that the area of the town was a semi-circle whose radius was 5,729.65 feet, with about 75% occupation. However, only six blocks were considered "within the fire limits." Most buildings were of frame, shingle roof construction, and "generally well-detached though in several instances blocks of small, one-story shingle roof dwellings are closely built up, making the danger from mutual exposure imminent." The report ended with a long list of improvements needed to secure a third class rating.

In contrast to the previous year's festivities, the 1916 Fourth of July celebration was reportedly a lively one. A swimming contest was held for men and boys in the river in front of the Officers Quarters at Fort Johnston. Spectators enjoyed a greased pig contest, a greased pole contest, a pie-eating contest, and a sack race. This year's inevitable baseball game was between Southport and Town Creek. The fireworks were postponed due to rain, but a dance was held at the Pavilion to close the activities.

In early 1917, Southport boasted of its "city hall." The city administration, with Thomas B. Carr as city tax collector, had its own offices on Nash Street, upstairs over the fire fighting equipment and next to the metal tower holding the fire alarm bell. Prior to that time, city affairs were conducted from various offices and places of business around the town which accounted for the loss of many city records in the 1915 fire.

Just as the new city hall was occupied, many Southport citizens viewed their first "airship." Hundreds gathered on the Garrison lawn to watch the performance of a hydroplane. Some were brave enough, and affluent enough, to take a 10-mile ride, declaring the fee of $15.00 per person was worth it.

Due to the developing national emergency, two chapters of the American Red Cross (one black and one white) were organized on April 2, 1917. Out of 140 chapters in North Carolina, two were in Southport. The chapters raised money, knitted socks, sewed bathrobes, rolled bandages, and arranged for beds to be available in Southport in the event of a bombardment of Fort Caswell. Four days after the chapters were organized, the United States declared war on Germany. Southport, as always, rallied to the cause.

June 5th was the official military registration day in the United States. The Brunswick County Court House was decorated with flags, bunting, and Red Cross emblems. In the afternoon, there was a patriotic parade as 184 Brunswick County men registered in the county. A number of men had already volunteered for service in the U.S. Coast Guard and were thus exempted from registration.

The *Charlotte Observer* declared, ''The Army which came into existence in America during the single day of June 5th is an Army born to conquer.''

The Fourth of July celebration that year was, of course, more patriotic than usual with many fiery orations. A parade of automobiles decorated with streamers of red, white, and blue were followed by marching units of Boy Scouts, Coast Guardsmen, Red Cross volunteers, and Camp Fire Girls. They were all marching to the music of the Fort Caswell Band. In the afternoon, the Caswell baseball team played the Wilmington Light Infantry team and the Red Cross Society served refreshments. The gaiety moved to the Pavilion in the evening for dancing and entertainment by the Fort Caswell Band.

The first draft call came on August 1st and the second just two weeks later. Thirty-five Southport men were drafted and they left on the Wilmington, Brunswick, and Southern (WB&S) Railroad for their training. Most were sent to Camp Jackson, S.C., for infantry training. When the United States entered the war, North Carolina's six National Guard units mobilized. The units had earlier trained at Caswell and were brought back to the fort, which was one of the State's two training camps. Several months later, one unit after another left for the battlefields of Europe and other units came to Caswell for training.

Happenings at Fort Caswell were of keen interest in Southport. Mrs. Minnie Ford Kotowski, now of Wyandotte, Michigan, was born at Fort Caswell and spent much of her childhood in Southport. She well remembers how events at Fort Caswell affected the daily lives of Southport people and particularly remembers that the citizens were notified in advance of target practice at Caswell. They would remove pictures and mirrors from the walls and dishes from the shelves because the firing of the big guns caused houses to shake. The noise, too, was deafening.

Gardens were very important to the war effort and were planted in every backyard and vacant lot as part of North Carolina's ''Feed Yourself'' campaign. At one Southport rally held for the purpose of encouraging the growing of gardens and field food crops, more than one hundred people stood when a count of home gardeners was taken. Families who did not have space for a backyard garden planted vacant lots or rented space in the ''Swamp Garden.'' This community garden was located in the swampy area along Bonnet's

Creek from Moore Street through to Leonard Street, and perhaps beyond.

Conservation of food and fuel was encouraged. Rationing, except for sugar, was voluntary, but the citizens were willing to comply and joined the rest of the nation in meatless, sweetless, and wheatless days. They cheerfully found substitutes as necessary.

At times the artillerymen at Fort Caswell outnumbered the town population, but Southport citizens decided to make life more pleasant for these men at the fort and those coming to shore from ships in port. The Masons offered the use of their building as a USO-type club on Franklin Square facing Nash Street and the citizenship responded generously. In a pamphlet by John R. Colter of the War Camp Community Service, he said, "The people gave deep from purse and heart to maintain a royal welcome for every man of the service who put foot on their soil." Town citizens worked together to raise money and solicit other gifts, and the Army-Navy Club officially opened. The *Wilmington Morning Star* of Saturday, September 1, 1917, stated:

ARMY AND NAVY CLUB AT SOUTHPORT IS NOW OPEN
THRONGS ATTEND CEREMONIES AT OPENING OF
HOME FOR SOLDIERS AND SAILORS

Southport, N. C. August 31. *The recently fitted up rooms on the entire first floor of the Masonic Lodge building on Nash Street were thronged last night by the soldiers of Fort Caswell and invited guests, who had been asked to attend the opening of the Army and Navy Club, these rooms being dedicated to the soldiers for their use whenever they may be in Southport, as a place where they may feel perfectly at home, to read the periodicals of the day, write letters, play games, smoke, and generally come and go as they please . . . and, as the name implies, the "boys" from Uncle Sam's war vessels that may be in these waters will be equally as welcome to the quarters provided.*

Local churches went to great lengths to make service men welcome. The ladies of St. Philip's Episcopal Church opened a lunch room called "The Dainty" on Howe Street near the waterfront where soldiers and sailors could get a home-cooked meal for a low price. Often men from the fort were invited to present special

Exterior of World War I Army-Navy Club.

Interior of World War I Army-Navy Club.

musical performances in the churches and Southport pastors acted as chaplains at Caswell. One soldier became choir director at the Southport Baptist Church. The pastor of that church, Rev. J.L. Jenkins, who was also the principal at Southport High School, was a favorite with the soldiers. He often went across the bay on the little government steamer *Getty* to hold services for them.

There were many pretty girls in Southport to be courted, and there was always some social activity in progress to which soldiers were invited. There were parties, oyster roasts, dinners, plays, and ballgames. World War I was a "singing war," with music used to keep up the morale of servicemen and civilians alike. There was mass singing in the training camps and at various activities with tunes as "Tipperary," "Over There," "There's A Long, Long Trail," and "Pack Up Your Troubles" heard over and over.

The music died for a while, though, as the Spanish influenza epidemic hit the lower Cape Fear in October and November of 1918 affecting almost every home in Southport. It was noted in the newspaper that the postmaster and all the postal clerks were sick at the same time in October. The schools and theater were closed by order of the Board of Health. Many church and civic meetings were canceled. The outlook was indeed gloomy at Fort Caswell where 500 cases of flu raged, and seven soldiers died. The Red Cross brought in a special nurse to care for the sick Puerto Rican laborers at the fort hospital, but more than 50 of the laborers died in spite of excellent care. The others were returned to Puerto Rico.

November 1919 brought one of the happiest days in Southport's history as peace was declared. News of the Armistice was quickly relayed. On the 11th, bells rang, whistles blew, hundreds of flags waved, and voices laughed, cried, sang, and gave thanks to God that the "war to end all wars" was over.

With the war over, Southport was elated to learn that the War Department planned to keep a permanent garrison of 1,550 officers and men at Fort Caswell. The town did not lose its spirit of enthusiasm and common purpose after hostilities ceased. They continued to maintain the Army-Navy Club as a community center for both the town and the men still stationed at Caswell. It became a place where adults could gather to spend leisure time, hold banquets and stage theatrical productions to raise money, or listen to lectures. The children were allowed to come after school, borrowing tennis nets and rackets, baseball gloves and bats, and basketballs (a novelty at the time). They could drink from the water fountain, also a novelty; play the big phonograph; and read books from the well-stocked library.

Shortly before World War II the Army-Navy Club ceased functioning. The east wing was removed, as was the bandstand and bowling alley. Some of the library's collection was given or sold to avid supporters, and other books were given to the public library located in the Officers Quarters Building at the Garrison. At some point a large wooden gymnasium had been added to the rear of the Masonic Lodge. The gymnasium was used for high school ballgames and community events until after World War II when it was torn down and replaced by a masonry building nearby facing Atlantic Avenue.

Excitement took place on May 3rd when an airplane flew over town dropping leaflets entitled "A Timely Message from the Clouds." This action was part of the Liberty Loan campaign to raise money to liquidate the country's enormous war debt. One of the leaflets was preserved by George W. Watson in the family scrapbook now in the possession of his daughter, Mrs. Elizabeth Griffin.

The Fourth of July passed rather quietly. The stores were closed, and families gathered for picnics at Fort Caswell, Bald Head, or in their yards. The reason for the low-key observance was that less than a month before a big event had taken place on Flag Day when a large, elaborate celebration was held honoring veterans of World War I, the Spanish American War and the Civil War. Flag-raising ceremonies, two parades, community singing, a banquet for the veterans, and a play staged at the Army-Navy Club were held. The lieutenant governor came from Raleigh to give the patriotic orations.

Following their summertime celebrations, it was back to routine for Southport. The coaling station began handling bunker coal for ocean-going vessels, a local packing company packed and shipped thirty freight cars of iced shrimp to all parts of the United States, and Dr. J. Arthur Dosher returned home to resume his practice.

Dr. Dosher, a Southport native, had been a captain in the American Expeditionary Forces. Upon his return to Southport, he became post physician for the U.S. Quarantine Service at the local station and set up an office for private practice in his home located at the corner of Moore Street and Atlantic Avenue. At times Dr. Dosher was also the only physician in the county. People traveled for miles to see him and he often made house calls. With no hospital facilities, many operations were performed in his office and at the Quarantine Office/Hospital on Bay Street. He was even known to have performed emergency operations on kitchen tables in private homes. An unusually skilled surgeon, he was widely acclaimed in his early years of practice for a delicate brain operation he performed under very difficult circumstances.

106

Dr. Dosher became one of the most beloved figures in the town's history. He was instrumental in bringing Brunswick County its first hospital and today J. Arthur Dosher Memorial Hospital in Southport is his living memorial.

Between Two Wars
1920-1940

As the Twenties—the Unforgettable Twenties—roared in, Southport was entering a short, prosperous period. It was a new age; the war was over; the survivors returned; and life was joyous again as the sorrows of war were erased. Pleasure seemed on everyone's mind. Couples danced the *Charleston*, and the radical new sounds of jazz were heard. Voices sang "Tea for Two," "I'm Sitting On Top of the World," and "Ain't We Got Fun," reflecting the high optimism of the day.

Many Southport women adopted the national trends of bobbed hair and short skirts. Even some of the reserved and conservative types gave in and escaped from the burden of long tresses. With no beauty parlor to visit, the ladies went downtown to Pack (Paxton) Tharp's Barber Shop to get their "boyish bobs," as some very short styles were called. Husbands and boy friends disapproved, but the short hair vogue among Southport women was not diminished.

During and immediately after the war, Southport's fame as a resort town spread. Visitors were enchanted by the "salubrious" breezes just as Joshua Potts had been more than a century before. The boarding houses were filled.

With Charles E. Gause, a descendant of a town founder, as its president, the Ocean Seafood Canning Company celebrated its fourth anniversary. This plant employed fifty people and was planning to enlarge its operations. A cold storage company was planned to transport fish to the West Indies and return with fresh fruits for distribution in Southport and nearby areas.

Circulation of books at the public library expanded. Reports state that 4,902 books were circulated during 1919 showing an increase of 358 books to the collection by gift or purchase.

The Great War strengthened the Woman's Suffrage movement, and by June 1920 Southport women were keenly interested. Mrs.

Anna Miller Davis was the first Southport woman to register to vote. In October, a women-sponsored citizenship lecture was held at the Army-Navy Club. This well-attended event was chaired by Mrs. Davis who introduced the speakers. Mayor J.W. Ruark, an attorney, read the voter registration laws and urged every woman to exercise their new privilege by registering and voting.

M.C. Guthrie, city official and civic promoter, declared that "the great anchorage basin at Southport is one of the distinguishing features of the port of Wilmington." And, once again, expressing the Southport dream, he continued, "The chief thing Southport wants is a coaling station . . . and this would serve the economic needs of both places." (The coaling stations "came and went.")

Southport's business district expanded. The growing tract included the area along Howe Street from Leonard Street to the waterfront and the older business block from Dry Street along Moore Street to its intersection with Howe Street.

The northeastern corner of Moore and Howe Streets (where Kirby's Prescription Center is now located) was, for some unknown reason, dubbed "Monkey Wrench Corner." The Loughlin building was located there where Jimmy Xanthos operated a restaurant. In the spring, summer, and fall, men gathered there to converse or to discuss business and civic affairs. When the weather became uncomfortable outside, the discussions were moved indoors. The second floor held the telephone office, presided over by Edna Dozier.

There were two drugstores facing each other on Moore Street—Watson's Pharmacy and Leggett's Drug Store. Other businesses found on Moore Street in Southport's business district were several dry goods stores, J.B. Ruark's General Store, two law offices, and the Post Office. Along Howe Street there was the Amuzu Theater, at least three grocery stores, and a butcher shop. The grocery stores were operated by John W. Lancaster, Willie Fullwood, and Dave Arthur; the butcher shop was run by Joel Moore. Farther north on Howe Street were two home dairies, Willie McKenzie's Ice Cream Parlor, and Mrs. Dollie Evans' store. The two latter stores were located near the intersection of St. George and Howe Streets. Mr. McKenzie's Parlor was a favorite of both children and adults as he made and sold homemade ice cream and sherbets. He also sold of cups of shaved ice covered with lavish helpings of grape, orange, and strawberry syrup. "Eatmores," a chocolate candy similar to today's Hershey's Kisses, were a childhood favorite at McKenzie's.

Mrs. Evans, an enterprising widow not only operated her general store, but hauled slabs from nearby sawmills, sawed them into stovewood lengths, and sold the truckloads around town as wood was needed for cooking and heating. A leader in the black community, Mrs. Evans was strongly influential in politics.

Two service stations that handled auto repairs operated on Howe Street. In addition to the grocery stores, small neighborhood stores served the needs of those who could not get downtown. One such store and restaurant was run by Walker Swain. The restaurant provided take-out service for his famous beef stew and potato pies.

The Post Office on Moore Street was Southport's leading social center where citizens gathered to wait until the mail was "put up." Although many families had post office lock boxes, others received mail from the General Delivery window. Everyone chatted until the General Delivery and stamp windows were opened and the day's business began. Mail came twice a day, but mornings were the favored time for socializing.

With soda fountains and seating space, the two drugstores were also favorite social centers. At Watson's Pharmacy and Leggett's Drug Store's soda fountains, ice cream cones and cherry and lemon-cokes sold for a nickel each. Milkshakes cost a little more. Not only could you get a prescription filled, but you could buy patent medicines, chewing gum, toilet articles, magazines, newspapers, tobacco products, and gift-boxed candies. Patrons sat at round tables on chairs with gracefully curved backs near the large windows which looked out on downtown Southport. Men gathered around the potbellied stove in the back room at Watson's Pharmacy discussing political affairs, such as the recurring effort to move the county seat from Southport. Until her health failed, the indomitable Kate Stuart could often be found at Watson's talking politics in the backroom instead of out front with the women and children.

The Miller Hotel, on Bay Street with an unobstructed view of the Cape Fear, was another social center. The lobby was used as the hotel dining room and a large soda fountain ran along one wall. Bedrooms were on the second floor.

Two boarding houses were on Bay Street, the Carolina House across Howe Street from the Miller Hotel and the Grimes House on East Bay Street. Much like the Stuart House, the Grimes House became a favorite place of visiting lawyers, judges, and tourists arriving on the steamer *City of Southport*.

110

Children especially liked "the Grove" in Franklin Square, with its lovely old live oaks towering over their playground. Here they played games, jumped rope, and created playhouses from the thick carpet of leaves. Sometimes families lost their yard rakes when the children failed to take them home after the day's activities. Using childhood imaginations, the leaves were raked to form dividing walls between "rooms" and to fashion beds, tables, and chairs. The boys, of course, were not often coerced into playing house so they played baseball games as the girls played house or school. The pump in "The Grove" furnished cool, clear, pure water to quench their thirst.

Another delightful place for young people and children in the summer was "Little Coney." Mayor C.L. Stevens recognized the need for a safe swimming area in the river and urged the city to approve it. This swimming area contained a pier, diving board, and float and was roped off in front of the Garrison House. Girl Scout troops and others from inland towns often came to enjoy swimming at "Little Coney."

In 1921 a bond issue provided funds for road improvements in Brunswick County. A major section of the sand-clay road running from Supply to Southport and was completed in 1923. This improved road made it easier to travel from other areas to the county seat for court or to handle county business. Mail service with other areas of the county also improved. In 1926 the road was widened and re-surfaced with a mixture of sand and asphalt.

In 1922, B.R. Page moved to Southport where he was employed as Superintendent of Schools with Miss Annie May Woodside as his assistant. The poorly financed school system in Brunswick County was very weak. In 1925, a bond issue passed for the building of five consolidated high schools. Southport High School was built on the corner of Nash and Dry Streets near the county courthouse. Years later the building was enlarged as the school population increased. This high school was used until 1969 when it mysteriously burned.

Before consolidation, the only high school in the county was in Southport, and high school students from many areas of the county came here for their education. Some, like Hazel Willetts of Bolivia, boarded with relatives or friends in town during the school week. Others traveled to and from school by automobile.

Also in 1925, the Brunswick County Training School, a high

school for blacks, was established on Lord Street in Southport. A.C. Caviness, a dedicated educator, served as principal of that school for 41 years. Upon integration of Brunswick's schools, the school's name was changed to Brunswick County-Southport High School.

Mr. and Mrs. Charles Lee were employed by the school system; Mr. Lee was custodian at Southport High School and Mrs. Lee was a well-liked and highly respected teacher at Brunswick County Training School. Their home, a two-story structure at the corner of Nash and Rhett Streets, became home for many boys and girls who came to attend Brunswick County Training School. Charlie Lee was a beloved figure among young and old in both white and black communities. Upon his retirement he was honored with a "Charlie Lee Day" at the Southport Baptist Church where he also served as custodian.

A major event of 1923 was the city's purchase of its first motorized fire truck. This fire engine carried two 30-gallon chemical tanks along with its hoses and reels. This truck served faithfully and efficiently until it was replaced by a larger truck in 1946. Originally, the truck was housed in an area beneath the city's administrative office on Nash Street in the edge of Franklin Square. When its days of usefulness were over, Southport merchant Dan Harrelson purchased the old truck as a keepsake. Later he returned it to the city as a gift. Through private donations and under the under the auspices of the Southport Volunteer Fire Department, the historic truck was authentically restored during the summer of Southport's Bicentennial year. In all its shining glory, it is now housed in a special section of the Fire House on Nash Street, a few yards from its first home.

Dreams die slowly in Southport; there was still hope the railroad would prosper and Southport would become a great port and coaling station. In September 1923, the Chamber of Commerce, with T.H. Lindsay as Secretary, requested that General E.F. Glenn prepare a "brief." This lengthy document, addressed to the State Ship and Water Transportation Commission "in behalf of Southport, N.C.," described in detail the reasons for making Southport the site of a state-owned and operated Port Terminal, and was submitted to the Commission. No action was taken but the matter was raised many times in the General Assembly by Brunswick County's Representatives. The WB&S Railroad (affectionately called the

"Willing But Slow" railroad) was still in operation in 1923 as Hubert M. Shannon moved his family from Wilmington to Southport to assume the position of Traffic Manager. Lottie Mae Newton of Southport was in charge of clerical work. Robert Shannon, son of the Traffic Manager, remembers his job with the railroad. He delivered all telegrams that came into the office over a direct line. Miss Lottie Mae, as she was called, took the messages, typed them, and handed them to Robert for delivery. Most of the messages concerned shipments to be made to New York from the fish and shrimp houses in Southport. Shannon also delivered the late weather bulletins from the U.S. Weather Bureau to Jessie Taylor. Mrs. Taylor than posted the telegrams for all to see on the bulletin board outside the Stevens Building on Moore Street. Robert's only compensation for his job came when there were telegrams to be delivered to yacht owners who had stopped in Southport for re-fueling their vessels. For these deliveries he was paid a nickel, which he quickly traded for an ice cream cone at Watson's Pharmacy.

In the late Twenties and early Thirties, "Cora Davis and Her Boys," were very popular. This lively, black band furnished music for Saturday night dances at the Miller Hotel and at the Black Cat Club which met upstairs in the Hood building at the corner of Moore and Dry (Davis) Streets.

Medicine shows, circuses, and fairs often came to town to furnish entertainment. Chautauquas came, too, with lectures and shows. Frequently, organizations such as the American Legion Auxiliary brought in outside troupes to stage musical productions as fund raising events.

In 1929 the stock market crashed, but its effects were not immediately felt in Southport and Brunswick County. That same fall, the problem of crossing Eagles Island to Wilmington from Brunswick County by slow ferry was solved with the construction of the "Million Dollar Twin Bridges" over the northeast and northwest branches of the Cape Fear River. The bridges were opened to traffic on December 10th, with great ceremony and free-flowing oratory. Dedication of the bridges stated:

> *To the patriotism of North Carolina's Soldiers and Sailors in the Great War Between the States, the Spanish American War, and the World War this bridge is dedicated on behalf of the whole people of the State of North Carolina.*

The Honorable C. Ed Taylor, Southport lawyer and legislator, was on four of the committees for the celebration, including the Executive Committee. He extended the welcome to Governor O. Max Gardner and guests on behalf of New Hanover and Brunswick Counties. Southport Mayor L.T. Yaskell and several other prominent citizens, Charles E. Gause, Thomas Lindsay, Joseph Ruark, Robert W. Davis, and Captain J.J. Adkins took part in the dedication ceremony.

With the opening of the new bridges and the highway improvements made, the rail line to Southport became unprofitable. Passenger service ended in 1933, and the freight service ceased in 1938. Then the WB&S began a bus service for passengers and mail which continued operations until after World War II.

Southport usually moved at a leisurely pace, but not all of the time. Four days in May 1930 (May 3-7) were busy, happy days for Southport folks. The 555-foot light cruiser, *USS Raleigh*, named for North Carolina's capital city, steamed into port and anchored in the Cape Fear River beyond the Government Dock. The ship, launched at Quincy, Massachusetts in 1922 and commissioned in 1924, was the second ship to bear this name.

Hosting the visit of the *Raleigh* was an ambitious undertaking for Southport. The ship had a complement of several hundred crew members and officers, roughly equal to about half the town's population of 1,600 persons. The occasion attracted thousands of visitors eager for a chance to board the ship. Food booths were set-up along the waterfront, in Franklin Square, and downtown. Children were delighted because many had never bought hot dogs and hamburgers from a food booth. Many organizations sold souvenirs and other items. Flags flew from every building and pole. The arrival of the *Raleigh* was an event remembered over the years.

Recorder's Court was held once a week and the week long Superior Court was held several times during the year. When court was in session, people thronged to Southport from all over Brunswick County and the state. For merchants and boarding houses this meant increased profits. The Grimes House on Bay Street was a favorite eating place as was the E. Sellers Cafe on Nash Street about a block from the courthouse. The Sellers establishment was particularly noted for its homemade beef stew. This establishment served as a gathering place for those attending court from Supply since many of them were relatives of Mr. Sellers.

Much social interaction took place in Southport. There was the pleasure of sitting on the front porch rocking or swinging while talking to your neighbor or others passing on the street. Almost everyone walked to his or her destination and there were lots of tourists. Adults had their organizations, bridge parties, dances, and church activities. Young people and children made candy, went looking for huckleberries and chinquapins in the woods, and gathered on the Garrison or at someone's home for singing and ghost tales. Churches played important roles in the social and spiritual life of the community. Youth leaders sponsored beach picnics, wiener roasts at "the Cliffs" on the river above town, and parties in the homes. Part of the fun was in walking to and from the parties in a group. Inevitably, youths paired off and held hands until his or her residence was reached. Those not holding hands clowned around, teasing those who did. Amateur theatrical productions continued to be staged in the high school auditorium.

Music and singing were important to all the social gatherings. Piano players were popular and had stacks of sheet music such as "It's Only a Paper Moon," "Lullaby of Broadway," and other easy-to-sing numbers. Magazines featuring words to the currently popular songs were collected. These were passed around, and the words were quickly learned.

Soon radios were in every Southport home and the air waves were filled with the romantic music of the Big Bands. Occasionally a big band came to Wilmington and groups of young adults traveled to Wilmington to dance. Kate Smith, who made her debut on radio in 1931, became the First Lady of Radio, bringing inspiration to all who heard her. She was a favorite in Southport.

At the Amuzu, Shirley Temple won the hearts of all who saw her on the silver screen. Fred Astaire and Ginger Rogers danced their way into Southport on the screen as they created their delightful routines. The "Gold Diggers" series, featuring Dick Powell and Joan Blondell, was popular with the romantically inclined. Board games such as "Monopoly" and jigsaw puzzles were popular family entertainments. In many homes there was usually a jigsaw puzzle set up on a card table, worked on at intervals by family and friends who visited. Miniature golf courses popped up around the country in the early 1930s and Southport's course was located on what was called "Front Street" (Moore) in the block between Howe and Dry (Davis) Streets.

115

The winter 1930-31 issue of the Wilmington telephone directory listed 76 telephones in the Southport section. The steady growth in the number of Southport phones is shown as there were 54 telephones listed in 1912 and 65 listed in 1926. The telephone added another social dimension to life in Southport.

June 2, 1930, was a memorable date for Southport and Brunswick County when the Brunswick County Hospital opened in Southport. This occasion was the result of hard work on the part of Dr. J. Arthur Dosher, J. Berg, C. Ed Taylor, Dr. R.E. Broadway, Dr. W.R. Goley, and others who saw the need for a county hospital. In 1935, the 55-bed hospital was incorporated and chartered under the joint ownership of Brunswick County and the City of Southport. C. Ed Taylor was elected Chairman of the Trustees. Money was scarce, and often it seemed the hospital would fail. The women of the Hospital Auxiliary sponsored many fund-raising events to bring in extra monies. One of the most popular events was their barbecue dinner which drew people from all over the county. In 1939, the hospital's charter was amended to rename the hospital the "J. Arthur Dosher Memorial Hospital" in honor of Dr. Dosher who had died in the hospital on January 11, 1939.

As the Great Depression deepened, Southport was caught in its strong grip. The price for shrimp dropped to $2.00 a bushel and those who headed them in preparation for packing were paid only a nickel a bucket. A "string" of fish, enough to feed a family, could be bought for twenty-five cents from the boys who were given the fish caught in shrimp nets. The boys met the shrimp boats, put the fish on strings, and then walked around town selling their wares. Business was brisk. Many evenings Southport families sat down to suppers of fried fish, grits, and hot biscuits or cornbread.

In 1915 an attempt was made to establish Southport as a shrimping port, but the idea was slow to catch on. Most local people did not think shrimp were fit to eat; they were more interested in oysters, clams, and fish. By the late twenties Southport attitudes changed and the town became a major shrimping port. Small trawlers pulled their nets along the ocean bottom and crews hauled the catch in by hand. The vessels brought the shrimp to the packing houses along the waterfront where they were headed, iced down, packed into rough wooden crates, and shipped to Northern markets either by refrigerated trucks or railway cars. At times, over seventy-five trawlers were bringing their catches into Southport.

Statistics show that the shrimp industry peaked in 1945 with an output of three million pounds. Some of those prominent in the shrimping industry were Lewis J. Hardee, Sr., William Wells, Sassa Fodale, and James A. Arnold, known as "Mr. Jim."

The Depression brought Southport's great "master carpenter" era to a halt as architectural activity waned considerably after World War I. Today the distinctive work of Henry Daniel, Joseph Daniel, W.T. Ottoway, A.E. Stevens, A.J. Robbins, and Price Furpless survives in the beautiful houses they built in town. A few commercial buildings were constructed in the 1920s, and a few bungalows were built in the mid-30s, but virtually no other building was done for a decade. A letter from a resident of Southport to a friend in Chicago described the economic situation in February 1933:

> Our fourth carload of Red Cross flour has been distributed about the county . . . The destitution is really appalling. Some have farm products, which cannot be sold, but can be eaten at home, and they have no clothing. And no work, except through Federal Relief, this just manual. Some are without food or clothing.

Then in November the letter-writer, a Red Cross volunteer, wrote:

> Almost daily yachts are here, enroute to Florida, and have been for a month or two. Seems early, but no doubt the rich want a change of scene and a chance to spend and live more luxuriously . . . The shrimp season continues, and the raw or "green" shrimp, peeled and packed in iced boxes, is hauled by truck to northern markets - 24 hours to place our shrimp in New York market. Saves a third in express charges, and 12 to 20 hours over rail transportation. What an age is this, but the wonderful highways make the change. Quite a fleet of trucks are on the move and gives a stir, locally, to several hundred working when none have had a job . . . The local Red Cross chapter is distributing clothing and some of that 'hog meat' that was slaughtered to save the price decline. I have little to do this year compared to a year ago.

Construction of the Intra-Coastal Waterway had an impact on Southport's economy. By June 1932, the waterway had been extended to Lockwood Folly and its construction meant jobs. Many Brunswick County men worked on the Southport-based dredges, *Blue Heron* and *White Heron*. Some of the men who did not live in

Southport boarded in town during the week, bringing in more money to strengthen the economy. The U.S. Corps of Engineers predicted that:

> *The construction of the waterway would permit the advantages of coast wise shipping to be brought to many places situated on interior routes which could not be served by ocean-going vessels . . . closing the gap between Southport and Georgetown would greatly add to the comfort and safety of private yachts, launches, and power boats, and the number making the trip would be increased.*

That prediction proved true as a long-lasting effect of the waterway was the creation of a yacht basin at the end of Brunswick Street providing a harbor for yachts, shrimp boats, and charter or party boats. The party-boat fishing business was pioneered in Southport by Hulan Watts and his wife, Annie Mae. Mr. and Mrs. Watts owned and operated several boats and other fishermen soon adopted sports-fishing as their business and Southport became a sports-fishing center on the coast.

After Franklin D. Roosevelt was elected to the presidency in 1933, some of the programs outlined in his ''Fireside Chats'' came to Southport. Two sewing rooms and a book binding operation provided work for many women. Work for the men was available when streets and roads were repaired and a public park was created beneath the beautiful oaks in Franklin Square. While this took away the favorite playground of the town's children, the work gave much needed jobs to their parents. Through the National Youth Administration several work projects were set-up for youth.

The Civilian Conservation Corps was organized in 1933. This emergency program salvaged the lives of many young men and saved much of the nation's natural resources. Camp 427, District B was established on June 12, 1933 in the Blue Ridge Mountains of North Georgia. In October of the next year, the company was moved to Southport where the men lived in tents until Camp Sapona on Leonard Street was completed. The well-trained, hardworking men immediately set about constructing truck trails, bridges, firebreaks, telephone lines, and two fire towers. Camp Sapona had the most complete woodworking shop in the District, the only blacksmith shop, and an unbeaten basketball team. Recreation at the camp included basketball, tennis, baseball, as well as reading from its library. Dances were held often, and many Southport girls attended.

Interior of barracks at Camp Sapona, 1934.

The camp, which remained open for thirty-eight months, did much for Southport and Brunswick County. Although most of the money earned was sent home to their families, the remainder was spent in Southport, giving the economy a needed boost. Both the town and county are still benefiting from the men's work in conservation and construction.

A few local men served at the camp, and others married Southport women and remained in Southport to start businesses. Some who had Southport connections were J.D. Ward, G.W. McGlamery, Homer Sherrill, Julian Southerland, C.L. Sellers, T.J. Hunt, Vallee Fredere, Louis Dixon, William Webb, C. Watkins, Fred Ashburn, Ivon Ludlum, Eugene Benton, Johnny Stiller, and John Ivey.

After being in business at the same location for 40 years, Dr. D.I. Watson retired on April 24, 1935, and sold Watson's Pharmacy to the W.E. Dosher family. The Doshers continued to operate the drugstore under the name Watson's Pharmacy.

Dr. Watson, then almost 79 years old, had come to Southport as a practicing physician in the late 1880s. After several years he discontinued his medical practice to become a full-time druggist and civic leader. The newspaper announcement of his retirement stated, ''The meticulous care with which he filled each prescrip-

119

tion, his wise counsel and genial personality made him one of the town's most popular citizens.''

Dr. Watson's retirement was announced in the first edition of *State Port Pilot* under the ownership and management of James M. Harper, Jr. The slogans of the newspaper were "Most of the News All of the Time" and "The Pilot covers Brunswick County". The *State Port Pilot* had been established in 1928 by W.B. "Bill" Keziah of Whiteville who became another Southport dreamer like Joshua Potts. The tough financial times of the Great Depression forced Mr. Keziah to relinquish management of the paper; it was sold to Mr. Harper, a young newspaper man from Raleigh. Mr. Keziah continued with the *Pilot* as reporter in spite of the fact that he was deaf and almost totally mute. Keziah was a great communicator and was well-known across the state as Southport's "One Man Chamber of Commerce."

Bill Keziah about 1935.

In the first Harper edition of the *State Port Pilot*, the society page (edited by Mrs. Warren Hood) carried news of a quilt exhibit by the Southport Woman's Club. Some of the quilts were more than a century old. The Elmore Motor Company of Bolivia advertised a "new Chevrolet" for $465, and Smith and McKenzie of Whiteville ran an ad that said:

We still have some mighty good mules on hand, and we know we can suit you if you are in the market for a mule. Cash or time. Hackney wagons.

Silk hose were on sale for 48 cents a pair, crepe was 50 cents a yard, and linen sold for 59 cents. Hats, "chic and matron styles," sold for 69 cents to $2.45. All sizes of overalls were going for $1 a pair and children's dresses went for 29 to 97 cents. The only newspaper in Brunswick County, the *State Port Pilot* carried news items from each section of the county. One column gave the names of hospital patients, and there were pages of club meetings, dances, theatrical productions, chicken suppers, school news, flower shows, engagements, weddings, and baby showers. Often house guests were mentioned in the paper, so everyone read the *Pilot* to know what was going on around the area.

On June 17, 1936, Southport and Brunswick County residents were issued an invitation, "We invite you to listen to a blow-by-blow account of the Louis-Schmeling fight Thursday night at the State Port Pilot office." A special rapport still exists between this newspaper and its readers. Although the chatty, personal columns and hospital news are no longer there, the same friendly atmosphere prevails. The paper is still owned by the Harper family and continues to support civic and political efforts that benefit the town. Its most popular column with longtime residents and newcomers alike is "The Way It Was," a photo with cut-lines from Southport's past.

On May 6, 1935, the Brunswick County Training School held its Field Day at the school on Lord Street. Certificates were awarded to the seventh graders, allowing them to graduate into high school in the fall. There were athletic events with Vashti Price, Lawrence Brown, Edgar Gore, Joseph Swain, Alicia Slade, and Louis Galloway winning various races. There were also literary contests and a parade. The week before, the white high schools in the county had held a similar Field Day in Franklin Square. The Field Day events were anxiously awaited each year when students promoted to high school were honored.

In June, the *State Port Pilot* announced that L.J. Dawkins, the well-loved and highly regarded principal of Southport High School, had resigned to take a similar position in Onslow County. Mr. Dawkins had served the Southport school since 1926.

Snow in Southport is a rare occurrence and has always made headlines. The heaviest snowfall to date was recorded on January 29, 1936, with a total of 6.5 inches. This snowfall broke the 1917 record of 4 inches. Snow-clearing equipment was non-existent, the school buses could not get into town, and other activities were hampered until the snow melted or could be shoveled. Cars and trucks were left idle, and people walked wherever they had to go. Although inconvenient for adults, the children and youth were understandably excited. Many had never seen snow except for a few flurries now and then, but never a snowfall that stayed on the ground long enough to make snowmen, eat snow cream, have snowball fights, and make pictures with their box cameras. The whole town was Christmas-card beautiful with its covering of snow.

In June 1936, an editorial in the *State Port Pilot* entitled ''Bonus Payments'' had this to say about an event important to many in Southport:

> *Salesmen and promoters have literally been 'licking their chops' in anticipation of the orgy of wild spending that they expect following the release on June 15 of the bonus bonds to veterans of the World War. We may be wrong but we believe that many of them are doomed to disappointment . . . the irresponsible youth who marched off to war in 1917 is now a man of 40 with a wife and kids.*

How prophetic this statement was. On June 15, the first bonds were delivered in Brunswick County through the Post Office Department. Charlie Dosher of Southport was the first Brunswick County veteran to receive his bonus. There was rejoicing throughout the county, not only by veterans and their families, but by all who were concerned about the state of the economy. There was very little reckless spending of the bonus money. Some veterans bought homes and farms, while others bought boats and nets to start a business. Some paid off heavy debts with part of their money and still others bought automobiles or trucks for the first time.

In 1936, Annie Mae Woodside was named Superintendent of Brunswick County Schools, the first woman in North Carolina to serve as superintendent of a county system. Miss Woodside, who had several years experience as Assistant Superintendent, served until her retirement in 1947.

In the winter of 1937, Southport was "famous" because of two of North Carolina's most-wanted criminals. While traveling from Southport to Whiteville a young Southport man, Robert Marlowe, and his fiancee, Mary Catherine Northrop, stopped on Highway 211 near Southport to help two men who had run into a ditch. The men insisted that Marlowe send his fiancee back to Southport with another motorist who had stopped to help and at gunpoint forced Marlowe to drive them to Hallsboro. Upon reaching Southport, Miss Northrop described the men to her father, law enforcement official M.A. Northrop, who recognized the kidnappers as William Payne and Wash Turner, escaped murderers and bank robbers. It was later learned that the men had lived for several weeks aboard a boat tied up in Southport's small boat basin. Southport and Marlowe were in the limelight again a few months later when Payne and Turner were captured and Marlowe testified for the prosecution at the trial. Both men were convicted and executed for their crimes.

In more mundane matters, the editor of the *State Port Pilot* was pleading with city officials to do something about the muddy streets. Very few streets were paved and drainage was so poor that after a heavy rain the streets were muddy for days. Tax revenues were low and the "Powell Bill" which now helps finance streets and roads had not been enacted.

Not many people were worried about the streets though. They were used to sand and mud and, given their current economic situation, were not anxious for a tax increase. They went about in their usual unhurried fashion, coping with inconveniences as necessary. The soft, soothing voice of Perry Como came to them over the airwaves. At the Amuzu the movie, *Mr. Smith Goes to Washington*, was a hit. Some Southport residents traveled to Wilmington to see Judy Garland in the new Technicolor sensation *The Wizard of Oz*. Also released shortly afterwards, was the four-hour *Gone With the Wind* that was to become one of the most famous movies of all time. Some Southport women, and perhaps even some of the men, saw the movie more than once, and it was talked about for weeks.

"Jitterbugging" was the dance of the day at school functions in the high school gym, on the stage, and at dances at the Caswell Beach Pavilion. Some have said that the dance was a way to express the mixed feelings of the times as the nation moved slowly out of the Great Depression and inexorable toward war. As the decade closed many Southport people felt that it was inevitable that sooner or later the United States would be drawn into the European troubles.

A Military Town In Another War
1941-1945

Southport entered the "Sweet and Sentimental Forties" with such tunes as "Anniversary Song," "Now Is the Hour," and "It's Been a Long, Long Time" being hummed and whistled. The town's citizens worked, played, and occasionally worried about world events. Salaries were low and jobs still scarce. Beginning stenographers were paid $6 for a five and a half day work week. School teachers were also poorly paid. Day laborers, household help, and shrimp house employees barely eked out a living. However, a young working girl could take her $6 pay check and leave Southport on Saturday afternoon at one o'clock and go to Wilmington on the WB&S bus. There she could shop in Wilmington's shops on Front Street, putting whatever she desired on layaway with small weekly payments. Coats and suits sold for as little as $12.95, and a hat sold for $2.98. Name brand shoes were sold for $7. With her shopping completed, she would return to Southport on the five o'clock bus.

Some Southport homes used electricity for cooking and heating water, but many still used oil cookstoves and woodburning ranges. Often a modern oil cookstove and a woodstove would sit side-by-side in a kitchen, with the woodstove used for slow cooking, baking, and heating water.

On September 16, 1940, the Selective Training and Service Act passed in Congress requiring men aged 21 to 35 to register for possible military training. Parents and wives were worried, as were young working men and those with young families. Rather than be drafted, some unmarried young men, especially those just graduating from high school, enlisted in their chosen branch of the armed services. In November, President Roosevelt, the Commander-in-Chief, was elected to an unprecedented third term.

The spring of 1941 brought the construction of the Wilmington shipyard, creating thousands of jobs for workers in the surrounding areas. The erection of hundreds of housing units for defense workers that were pouring into Wilmington meant still more available jobs. Carpenters, masons, electricians, and plumbers were in demand and employers were begging for clerical employees. Many Southport laborers commuted to Wilmington to work. Pulpwood companies bought huge tracts of timber in Brunswick County which added large amounts of money to the economy. Lawyers at the county seat benefitted as they researched property titles and prepared legal instruments for the timber transactions. A prominent attorney in Southport during this time, S. Bunn Frink, joined the U.S. Coast Guard and became Captain of the Port of Wilmington.

Any lingering vestige of the Great Depression gave way to the upsurge in the economy as Southport citizens obtained work in the abundant, well-paying jobs. The increased income allowed those who were renting to look toward home ownership. However, the scarcity of building materials for the civilian market brought those dreams crashing down.

In May 1941, the Sacred Heart Catholic Church on Caswell Avenue was dedicated. Member Mark Connaughton, in his history of Catholicism in Brunswick County, related that in prior years, Southport's Catholics had worshipped in several different places. They first met in homes serving as missionary outposts with priests from St. Mary's in Wilmington leading the services. The Shannons, McNeils, Marrans, Malarkeys, and others hosted the services. Later, the congregation held their services at the Civilian Conservation Corps camp on Leonard Street. In 1937 the worshippers moved to an upstairs room in what was called ''The Community Center'' (now Franklin Square Art Gallery). Sacred Heart Church has grown and members and visitors worship in a new, splendid edifice on N.C. Highway 211 at Dosher Cut-off Road.

With increasing submarine activity along the North Carolina coast, the protection and defense of the United States became a critical issue in Washington. On November 17, 1941, the U.S. Navy purchased from Caswell-Carolina Corporation the 248.8-acre Fort Caswell reservation. This property was to be used for training, for communications, and as a submarine tracking station. Once again Fort Caswell was to play an important role in the life of Southport.

December 6, 1941, was ''the last day of peace, a final day of innocence" for Southport as well as all America. Many hoped that war could be averted, but fear overrode that hope. However, with only sixteen shopping days until Christmas and with holiday preparations, fears were put aside for the moment. Business was brisk on Moore and Howe Streets, and some shoppers traveled to Wilmington for purchases. Nylon stockings had reached the market and were coveted as Christmas presents—if they could be found. The *Lucky Strike Hit Parade* was the favorite radio show on Saturday night and "Chattanooga Choo-Choo" was near the top of the list.

Within hours Southport's peaceful existence ended. The following day the news came that Japan had made a devastating air attack on Pearl Harbor. Two Southport men, brothers Frank and Bryant Potter, were stationed at Pearl Harbor aboard the Cruiser *USS Helena*. They survived the attack. Many Southport men were already in service, some at Fort Bragg and some at other military bases. Most of Southport's citizens who remember that "day of infamy" also remember exactly where they were when they heard the awful news. From that day forward, life in Southport changed drastically, never to return to the old ways.

The war was constantly on peoples' minds and in their hearts; "Remember Pearl Harbor" was the rallying cry. More Southport men and women joined the labor force. Housing became a problem as wives and families of servicemen at the Caswell Section Base and Oak Island Coast Guard Station arrived in town to be near their loved ones.

People who owned rental property did all they could to meet the increased demand for housing. They enlarged their buildings to create more living space and made apartments out of existing space. Homeowners crowded their families into fewer rooms and rented out the vacant space thus created. Quite often the beautiful porches of Southport's historic homes were enclosed to make rentable living quarters. Fifty years later, in a letter quoted in Southport Historical Society's newsletter, *Whittlers Bench*, Mrs. Wanda Golden, a war bride in Southport, wrote:

> *I remember we lived at Miss Louise Watson's on the left hand side of the hall in one big room. Later we moved across the hall to two rooms. I washed clothes on a scrub board and cooked on a kerosene stove.*

Workers were constantly recruited for job openings in Wilmington. With gasoline and tires rationed, car pools were formed; rarely did a private automobile make the trip to Wilmington without several riders. WB&S Railroad Company ran buses from Southport throughout the county and to Wilmington on a daily basis. Old school buses were used to transport shipyard and construction workers to Wilmington around the clock. Some Southport men worked at Camp Davis in Holly Ridge, Fort Bragg in Fayetteville, Bluethenthal Airfield in Wilmington or at Camp Lejeune in Jacksonville.

During the first half of 1942, German U-boats sank so many oil tankers and other vessels off the North Carolina coast that the area became known as "Torpedo Junction." On March 16, the *Wilmington Morning Star* carried a lead article about the oil tanker *John D. Gill* which had been torpedoed off Southport. Survivors and bodies of the dead were brought into Southport. For security reasons and by orders of Navy Secretary Knox the names and number of survivors and the exact date of the tragedy were not revealed.

Dosher Memorial Hospital was placed on a wartime footing. The Auxiliary Nursing Corps, well-trained by Registered Nurse Mary M. Fergus, nursed the survivors. Leila H. Pigott of Southport, a member of the Corps, vividly remembered the event. The bodies of the men who had died of burns or drowning were taken to Kilpatrick Funeral Home for identification. Those bodies with identification papers in their clothing were sent home. Surviving shipmates identified all except four of the others. These four men were given a funeral service at Kilpatrick Funeral Home and they were buried in unmarked graves on city-owned lots set in Northwood Cemetery.

One of those identified by name only was a 21-year-old Filipino mess boy who had drowned. His death certificate, dated March 29, 1942, has this notation:

> *No information obtainable as to personal history. The body was identified by survivors of the sunken tanker John D. Gill.*

He, too, was buried in Northwood Cemetery.

Dosher Memorial continued to operate under wartime conditions including blackouts, rationing, and air raid drills. Dr. L.C. Fergus carried a heavy case load in his office in addition to his service at the hospital. Dr. Landis G. Brown, the town's other doctor, was called into service by the Navy Medical Corps.

Blackout orders were in effect in late April, and citizens were warned to stay away from strange-looking objects that could be bombs on area beaches. The U.S. Coast Guard maintained a mounted horse patrol along the Brunswick County coast to provide security against spies and fifth columnists possibly coming ashore at night from German submarines.

Again, Southport was a military town. The Coast Artillery set up a Search Light battalion on the Garrison. Army troops were stationed at Camp Sapona, the old CCC camp on Leonard Street. Across the bay were the Caswell Section Base and the Oak Island Coast Guard Station. Bald Head was virtually deserted except for a few Coast Guardsmen and horse patrol units. Close by were troops at Bluethenthal Air Field and at Camp Davis. Men from all the locations were often in Southport.

A few Southport women enlisted in the service. Blue stars on white flags appeared in home and store windows, honoring sons or husbands in service. The only Gold Star was for Captain Churchill Bragaw who was killed in action in Italy. Eager for news, people played their radios day and night and subscribed to the *Raleigh News & Observer*, the weekly *State Port Pilot*, and to both morning and evening editions of the Wilmington newspapers. Letters from servicemen were shared by family and friends. Using a typewriter from E.J. Prevatte's law office and the mimeograph machine from Mrs. Ressie Whatley's office, a youth organization at the Southport Baptist Church published a newspaper for servicemen known as *The Short Circuit*. Copies were mailed to servicemen whose addresses could be obtained by the young reporters and editors. Each issue contained news about those servicemen including their addresses so they could stay in touch with one another.

The American Red Cross recruited volunteers throughout the county to make surgical dressings. The Southport team met in the Masonic Lodge to roll hundreds of bandages. All residents wanted to play a part in the war effort, no matter how small. Not only did they roll bandages, volunteer at the hospital, and share their homes, they also planted Victory Gardens in their yards and recycled scrap rubber, metal and fats. Few grumbled as tires, gasoline, sugar, coffee, leather shoes, and other items were rationed. They accepted what was available, knowing that every bit saved meant more for their fighting men.

With ration coupons for meat in short supply, chicken and

seafood were the main courses for many meals. Wartime cookbooks such as *Your Share* and *Coupon Cookery*, along with magazine articles, gave tips for stretching ration points. There were recipes for baked Spam, dried beef dishes, and "Emergency Steak." There was even a recipe for a wartime cake that contained no eggs or milk and only a small amount of sugar and vegetable shortening. Vegetables from Victory Gardens were mainstays for the cooks, and dried beans and biscuits were popular in Southport as they had always been.

On the fashion scene, Southport citizens used the clothes already in their wardrobes as long as they could. Materials were scarce and garments often had to be remodeled, but skilled seamstresses found inventive ways to do so. When clothing was purchased, the women bought tailored suits with nipped-in waists and padded shoulders. Some favored two-piece dresses with flouncy peplums, and the shirtwaist dress was in vogue, especially for office wear. Sweaters were very skimpy; hats and gloves were necessities. Sometimes women preferred to paint their legs to resemble stockings rather than to wear dowdy hose of rayon or lisle. The recently invented nylon had gone to war and silk was unavailable. Men wore "snowflake" sweaters and two-piece suits without pleats or cuffs. Of all the substitute items, shoes were probably the most unsatisfactory. Leather shoes were restricted to three pairs a year; the unrationed shoes were ugly, made with cloth tops and cardboard or thin wooden soles and heels. The ladies could not count on the heels staying on the shoes, either.

The military town of Southport gained a "Federal Community Building," which was operated by the United Service Organizations. The dedication of the USO building, located on the Garrison grounds, was held April 25, 1942, and was hosted by the Defense Recreation Committee of Brunswick County. The officers of the governing board of the USO Citizens Committee were Mrs. James E. Carr, chairman; L.T. Yaskell, vice-chairman; and E.J. Prevatte, secretary. W.S. Wells was chairman of the Defense Council.

Movies, table games, dances, and other entertainment were available at the USO and town citizens and servicemen were invited to take part. Southport women served as volunteer hostesses to assist paid personnel. A corps of volunteers also manned the phone line in the USO building. If an air raid alarm sounded, they would transmit messages for relay to defense officials of Southport.

Other fun times were available for the young people, too. Movies were seen at the Amuzu. Buses left regularly from the post office on weekends to take young people to Caswell Section Base for movies and ballgames with the servicemen stationed there. Churches gave parties and had Sunday night fellowship hours. Servicemen were invited into Southport homes for meals and family activities. There were ballgames played in Southport as well as at Caswell. Often groups of young people gathered in the kitchen at Oak Island Coast Guard Station in the evening to make candy or pop corn. With these simple fun times, the thought of war was pushed into the background for a few hours.

In August 1942, Southport was saddened by the death of native son Superior Court Judge Edward H. Cranmer, Jr. Appointed to the bench in 1920 by Governor Thomas Bickett, Judge Cranmer served the State of North Carolina well. His early career was spent as an attorney and civic leader in Southport and a North Carolina Senator in Raleigh. Respected and well-liked by his colleagues, he was known for his fairness and humanitarian spirit in every city and town where he held court.

C. Ed Taylor was appointed by North Carolina to serve as County Collector of War Records. Mr. Taylor, always interested in history, took his new duties seriously and began the collecting task immediately. According to the Coordinator of Records in Raleigh, Mr. Taylor made a significant contribution to North Carolina's program of collecting records of the "valued endeavors on the home front."

In mid-1943, the war intensified as the Allies strengthened. In most Southport homes, a world map occupied a wall and was studied daily as news of troop movements came by radio and newspaper. D-Day, the Normandy beach landing, occurring on June 6, 1944, and was the most outstanding event of the war to that time. The elation of Allied victory was dulled by sadness as fearful families found themselves awaiting possible telegrams from the War Department.

In the belief that the war would soon be over, the U.S. Congress passed the Serviceman's Readjustment Act, or what was known as the G.I. Bill. This bill was later to help many of Southport's fighting men.

On August 1, 1944, thoughts were momentarily diverted from the war as a hurricane with 80 mile-per-hour winds approached. The beaches were evacuated and two U.S. Coast Guard cutters capsized and sank as they protected a Liberty Ship which had just been torpedoed near shore. There was much waterfront damage as the storm struck the coast near Southport. A month later another hurricane of lesser intensity struck before the town had fully recovered from the previous one. This was exciting to the servicemen and their families because it was their first encounter with tropical storms.

In the November presidential election President Roosevelt won an unheard of fourth term, with Harry S. Truman as his vice president. In spite of Allied gains, it seemed to Southport citizens that the long war would never end. On April 12th of the next year, the ailing President Roosevelt died at his residence in Warm Springs, Georgia. Mr. Truman was sworn-in as events in the European Theater of Operations, under the command of General Dwight D. Eisenhower, were escalating. On May 8, 1945, word reached around the world that Germany had formally surrendered to General Eisenhower. V-E Day had come; in Southport homes and churches there were prayers of thanksgiving and joyous celebration as families hoped for their men's quick return from the European battlefields. Fervent prayers appealed for a quick victory in the Pacific as well.

Even as the men who had fought in Europe resumed their civilian life, the astounding news came of atomic bombs dropped on Hiroshima on August 6, and on Nagasaki just three days later. August 14 was the long-awaited V-J Day. Japan's formal surrender to General Douglas MacArthur aboard the *USS Missouri* in Tokyo Bay came on September 2nd.

The war over, Southport was no longer a military town. The armed forces moved out, and the war survivors came home to a triumphant America, now the world's number one nation. Some of Southport's young people had married and gone elsewhere to live. Others came home to find themselves unemployed; jobs created by the defense industries no longer existed. There was fishing and shrimping, but sales prices were low. Attending college and trade schools under the G.I. Bill was an alternative for some of the veterans. Many had dreamed of taking up life where they had left off in 1942, but that was not to be. Inevitable change had come; Southport was never again the quiet, sequestered fishing village of pre-war days.

Epilogue

Five years after World War II, the Federal Government declared Fort Caswell surplus property. Put on the open market, the property was purchased by the North Carolina Baptist State Convention for use as a religious retreat and conference center. The new owners have preserved and restored much of the site's long history.

Following the war, sports fishing in Southport increased dramatically with the charter boat fleet numbering fifteen at one time. Every summer and early fall weekend the boats were chartered. Half of the bookings were referrals from Annie Mae Watts. Her husband, the late Captain Hulan Watts, known as "Crow," and his brother, Doonie, are credited with starting party boat fishing in Southport during the Depression when Southport became a mecca for sports fishing enthusiasts. W.B. Keziah, newspaper reporter and one-man chamber of commerce, predicted and publicized Southport's sports fishing and the town's competent, dependable boat operators. This established Southport's reputation among anglers. In May of 1988, at a banquet held at the Sandfiddler Restaurant, Mrs. Watts, then 85 years-old and still booking charters, was presented a Small Business Award for her family-owned business. At the same banquet a Small Business Award was made to the McCoy-Greene Funeral Home, another family-owned business. Mrs. Watts stated that when she first started booking fishing parties she had to use the telephone at the McCoy-Greene Funeral Home. In those days there were not many telephones in Southport and neighbors helped each other.

In 1952, Southport secured a building supply business when E.C. Blake of Cumberland County, seeing the need, purchased a site at the Sawdust Trail intersection and established the small, family-owned Blake Builders Supply. This was the first builder's supply in Southport since the late 1880s. The business grew quickly, and the original building was expanded several times before a large modern store was constructed. After Mr. Blake's death, the business eventually changed ownership.

Wilmington's first television station came on the air in 1953; television sets soon became commonplace in Southport homes, further erasing any lingering isolation from the outside world. Adults could enjoy Uncle Miltie, Lucy, and *The Edge of Night*. This soap opera became so popular in Southport that citizens were known to leave their offices and stores to go home to watch the program. The youngsters eagerly waited for *Howdy Doody Time*; occasionally a teacher or parent took a group to Wilmington to appear on TV as Howdy Doody fans. The little "baby boomers" read dozens of the popular, affordable *Little Golden Books* while the adults read the daring new novels *Forever Amber* and *Peyton Place*.

The Town of Long Beach was incorporated in 1953. Long Beach, together with Yaupon Beach and Caswell Beach, were experiencing a tremendous growth as families began to establish permanent homes on Oak Island. This beach growth had a strong effect on Southport schools, churches, professions, and businesses.

October 15, 1954, has never been forgotten by any citizen living here on that date. Hurricane Hazel hit the town and county with a double whammy after rambling around in the tropical Atlantic

Southport's waterfront after Hurricane Hazel.

134

for several days. Gusts as high as 200 miles-per-hour were recorded at the Oak Island Coast Guard Station before weather instruments failed. Sustained winds were officially estimated at 140 miles-per-hour. Although no Southport lives were lost in the storm, the wind and rain damage was devastating as Hazel lashed the coast for many hours. All twenty of the town's fuel docks were demolished and piled on shore; all of the shrimp packing houses were also destroyed. Waterfront stores and restaurants were damaged, some beyond repair. The majestic old Stuart House on Bay Street was one of the storm casualties. Streets were flooded, boats washed ashore, and mighty trees were uprooted.

At Long Beach only five of the 357 structures were left standing. Streets and roads were obliterated and the utility poles blown away. As viewed along the oceanfront after the storm, the scene was almost primeval with only the sand, the sea, and the wind where just the day before had been a bustling beach town.

Years later, as predicted by Art Newton, local photographer and artist, in his book *Hurricane Hazel, The Great Storm in Pictures*, citizens were still saying, "Oh, that was before Hazel," or "That happened right after Hazel."

In August of the following year, while damages from Hurricane Hazel were still being assessed and damages repaired, two more hurricanes, Connie and Diane, hit Southport within a week of each other. A month and two days after Diane struck, later Hurricane Ione blasted her way into Southport. Sustained winds in these three hurricanes ranged from 70 to 74 miles-per-hour. Flooding and erosion caused tremendous damage to the already severely battered coast.

A month after the three hurricanes had faded into history, an event took place a few miles up river that was to have a lasting and beneficial effect on Southport and the surrounding area.

On October 19, 1955, the United States Army Corps of Engineers and Transportation Corps held a joint dedication ceremony and open house for the new Sunny Point Army Terminal. Today this installation is known officially as the Military Ocean Terminal at Sunny Point (MOTSU), but to local citizens it will always be "Sunny Point." Music for the special occasion was furnished by the 440th Army Band of Fort Bragg and the invocation was offered by the retired Major General Ivan L. Bennett, a native of Brunswick County and former Chief of Chaplains of the U.S. Army. Brigadier General

James Glore, Commanding General of the Atlantic Transportation Terminal Command, welcomed the gathering. Southport's Mayor Roy Robinson and Wilmington's Mayor Dan Cameron brought greetings from the two cities. North Carolina Governor Luther B. Hodges was on hand to bring a message of welcome from the state. The main address was made by the Honorable F. Ertel Carlyle, U.S. Representative for the 7th Congressional District. Colonel William A. McAleer, the first commanding officer of the new facility, was master of ceremonies.

Construction of the terminal which began in December 1952, was completed shortly before the 1955 dedication ceremonies. The facility was the first in the nation built for loading ammunition which "met the proper quantity-distance requirements," according to officials.

The Sunny Point installation greatly boosted the economy of Southport and Brunswick County. New jobs were available and the Transportation Department employees who had transferred to Sunny Point made their permanent homes in Southport. In October 1975, as part of the celebration of Sunny Point's Twentieth Anniversary, the Southport Board of Aldermen unanimously adopted a resolution expressing appreciation for Sunny Point and its contribution to the Southport community. The resolution further spoke of those who had come to Southport with the terminal as "now interwoven into the religious, social, and civic facets of the community."

Today MOTSU ships more military equipment and ammunition than any other terminal in the United States. Employing 300 people from Wilmington, Boiling Spring Lakes, and the Southport-Oak Island area, the payroll and other benefits help stabilize the area's economy. The commanding officer and four enlisted senior personnel and their families live on old Fort Johnston, thus making Fort Johnston one of the oldest forts in the nation still in use.

Southport is still a military town just as the area was a military site in 1792 when the founders arrived.

As the writer, Rita Mae Brown, has said: "The closer one gets to one's own time, the harder it is to see it clearly." How true.

It is quite impossible to make an evaluation of the events that have occurred in Southport from the close of World War II to the present. That must be done by future writers. However, brief men tion can be made in this story of the later forces and events that have affected the town's destiny.

Joshua's dream became reality beyond what he envisioned in those heady days from 1792 to 1825. However, tourists still come in large numbers for the same reason—to enjoy those same "salubrious breezes" that cured his "debilitating fever" and gave him the urge to lay-out a town around the Fort. These tourists come and enjoy the climate, the sights, and the people; they return to their homes and tell others. They continue to return again and again. No longer is Southport an unknown dot on a North Carolina map, or a "jumping off place", as some once called it.

Now not only are there tourists, but retirees and others looking for a new home have found it in Southport. Houses in the historic district have been purchased and restored. The town limits have been expanded several times to take in more residences and businesses. Large industries such as Carolina Power and Light Company, Pfizer Corporation (now Archer Daniels Midland Company), and Cogentrix came and established plants that employed local residents These companies brought economic growth which Southport had never before experienced or even imagined.

Appendix

LAWS OF NORTH CAROLINA
SESSION OF 1792
- - - - - - -
Chapter LXII

AN ACT TO LAY OFF AND ESTABLISH A TOWN NEAR FORT JOHNSTON, ON THE WEST SIDE OF CAPE FEAR RIVER IN BRUNSWICK COUNTY.

Whereas it has been represented to this General Assembly by the pilots, and a number of other inhabitants of Brunswick county, that the erection of a town on the west side of Cape Fear river, will be attended with a variety of beneficial effects to the health, commerce and convenience of said county and those adjoining:

I. Be it therefore enacted by the General Assembly of the state of North Carolina, and it is hereby enacted by the authority of the same, That after reserving all the land near the said Fort Johnston, which the Commissioners hereinafter appointed may deem necessary for the future defence thereof, and also one acre of ground for each of the pilots or their widows, agreeable to an act passed at Hillsborough, in the year of our Lord one thousand seven hundred and eighty four, one hundred and fifty acres be appropriated for a town; and that the said land be, and is hereby vested in Benjamin Smith, William Espy Lord, Robert Howe, Joshua Potts and Charles Gause, Esquires; who are hereby appointed and constituted Commissioners and Trustees for laying out and directing the building and carrying on the said town; and the said Commissioners, or a majority of them, are hereby authorized and required to lay out a town containing one hundred lots, to consist of half an acre each or thereabouts, with convenient streets and squares; which lots, streets and squares are hereby constituted and erected a town, and shall be called and known by the name of Smithville; and the overplus of land shall remain as a common for the use of the said town, except the skirts on the water, which the Commissioners may hire out for the benefit of the said town: And the Commissioners, or a majority of them, shall have full power and are hereby required to make, or cause to be made, a fair plan of said town, and mark or number each lot therein; and after reserving ten lots for the use of said town, shall take subscriptions for the remainder of such persons as may be willing to subscribe for the same, and when a sufficient number of lots shall in their opinion be subscribed for, the said Commissioners shall appoint a day, and give public notice thereof for drawing said lots, which shall be done by ballot, in a fair and open manner, by the direction and inspection of a majority of said Commissioners; and each subscriber shall be entitled to the lot or lots drawn for him or her, and corresponding with the mark or number contained in the plan of said town; and the said Commissioners, or a majority of them, are hereby empowered to grant good and sufficient titles in fee simple, for said lots, at the cost of the subscribers. Provided that no one person shall be permitted to subscribe for more than six lots for his or her own use.

II. And be it further enacted by the authority aforesaid, That in case of refusal, death or removal out of the county of any of the Commissioners appointed by this act, the remaining Commissioners are hereby empowered and required to appoint from time to time, some other person or persons who has, or have an house or houses in the said town, or are resident in the said county, in the place of him or them so refusing, dying or removing; and the now Commissioner or Commissioners so appointed, shall have the like power and authority in all matters and things, as if he, or they had been expressly named and appointed by this act.

III. And be it further enacted, That the first meeting of the Commissioners, shall be held on the fourth Saturday in January next, when they shall, and may appoint a Chairman and town clerk, and thereafter such other officers, as shall appear to them necessary; that the town clerk shall give bond with sufficient security, for performing the duties of his office; and on the settlement of his accounts annually, and punctually paying the monies for which he is liable, he shall be allowed such commissions, fees or salary, as the Commissioners deem reasonable; he shall keep a town book, in which shall be entered the time of subscribing, or taking the entries of lots, the names of the subscribers, and the mark or numbers of the lots subscribed for, orders made by the Commissioners, the time when deeds are granted, an account of the monies received, the manner of applying the same, the sums remaining on hand, and all other matters properly relating to his office.

IV. And be it further enacted, That each respective subscriber for any lot in said town, within one month after it shall be ascertained to whom each of the said lots doth belong, shall pay, and satisfy to the town clerk, two pounds for each and every lot by him subscribed for; and in case of refusal, or neglect to pay the same, the town clerk may, and shall in his own name, sue for the same, and after receiving the said subscription money, and deducting so much as is necessary and reasonable for the expense and trouble of laying off the said town, which charges shall be presented and approved by the county court before they shall be allowed as vouchers; the said town clerk is hereby required to pay the balance to the treasurer of the University, for the use of the same.

V. And be it further enacted, That the Commissioners of the said town shall be vested with, and are hereby declared to have power from time to time, to pass any order they may judge proper, for promoting the good and safety of the said town, and the proper regulation thereof and also to possess all authorities given by the laws of this state to the Commissioners of other towns; and in all their acts a majority shall constitute a quorum, nor shall they do business with a less number; and the said Commissioners are hereby required to fix up a state of their accounts, at the most public places of said town, on the first Monday in August, in every year; and from time to time to call to account all persons, for any monies which may, or ought to be in their hands, belonging to the said town; and in case of their failure or refusal to pay, to bring suit for all such monies, which shall be applied as a majority of the Commissioners may think most conducive to the emolument and advantage of the said town.

Read three times, and ratified in General Assembly this 31st day of December, 1792.

REMARKS MADE BY 17-YEAR-OLD SOPHIA DREW,
DAUGHTER OF MR. AND MRS. JESSE DREW,
AS SHE PRESENTED A FLAG OF THE CONFEDERACY
TO THE SMITHVILLE GUARD IN 1861.

"Officers and Gentlemen of the Smithville guards:

Standing on this beautiful greensward, with gay uniforms before me, and smiling faces around me, memories of the past crowd thick upon the mind. This soil was once crimsoned with the blood of our Revolutionary sires. 'Twas here that General Ashe at the head of our brave Militia drove out our British foes from old Fort Johnston.

Remember, Gentlemen, that upon the soil of Old Brunswick the first armed resistance was made to British Tyranny. Every foot of our soil is hallowed by the memories, and illustrated by the deeds of Moore, Ashe, Howe, Harnett and Waddell and a host of others equally brave of whose names and deeds history makes no mention. Their fame is your richest heritage. Oh! preserve and perpetuate it.

With this injunction, the ladies of Smithville, whose honored Representative I am, present you with this flag. We know you will bear it bravely, for the soil of Brunswick does not produce cravens.

You have our earnest prayers for success in all the affairs of life. We trust that sweet peace may ever smile upon our favored land. But should the stern war cry come, whether from Europe's monarchy or from the demons of Northern fanaticism, remember your motto and 'maintain your Constitutional rights at all hazards.'

> Strike-till the last armed foe expires!
> Strike-for your altars and your fires!
> Strike-for the green graves of your sires,
> God, and your native land.

Should this dire calamity befall us, the Women of Brunswick place their lives and honor in your keeping.

Come back to us as conquerors, and we will bind the laurel around your brows. But should numbers overpower you, fall with

144

<u>your faces to the foe</u>; and we will cherish your memories as household words. We will bedeck your graves with flowers and water them with our tears.

Your graves will become Pilgrim Shrines, and our matrons will take their children there and reciting to them your glorious deeds, teach them how brave men die.

I now resign this flag to your keeping.

(The underlined words were underlined in the original script)

Copied from

*REPORT OF THE SECRETARY OF THE NAVY
TO CONGRESS, 1865*

Report of Lieutenant Wm. B. Cushing.

United States Steamer Monticello,
Off Fort Caswell, N.C., January 31, 1865.

Sir: In obedience to your order of the 17th instant, I proceeded to the western bar to ascertain the state of affairs in that quarter. On the morning of the 18th I pulled in to Fort Caswell to demand its surrender, and finding it abandoned, hoisted a flag there, as well as on the other forts at the mouth of the harbor. I then proceeded with four men to the town of Smithville and received its surrender from the mayor, mounted rebels leaving the town at the same time. I hoisted our flag on the battery at that point, which, with the barracks and public property, was uninjured. Captured several hundred stand of rebel muskets, with some of which I armed my men, at the same time sending one sailor and four negroes in a boat for re-enforcements. We held the town with three men until their arrival. The inhabitants mostly remained in their homes, and by their behavior impressed me with the idea that they had been rebels, but were beaten back into loyalty. We also captured a considerable quantity of commissary stores, the next day vessels came down from above, and one hundred and fifty sailors were sent on shore to garrison the town, of which I retained command until relieved by the army, one week after. In the meantime I sent down boats, crews and officers, nightly, to tend the range lights on the beach, and attempt to decoy in blockade runners. On the second night we were awarded by the arrival of two steamers, the "Stag" and "Charlotte", that came over the bar and stopped off the wharf, signalling to Fort Caswell. Nor receiving the expected answers from the fort, they were about to turn back, when they were hailed by Acting Ensign Huntington of the Monticello, who told them the signal corps had been withdrawn, and it was all right—to go on up to Smithville. Following this advice, they fell into our hands.

I am, sir, very respectfully, your obedient servant,

W.B. CUSHING
Lieutenant Commanding U. S. Steamer Monticello

Rear-Admiral D.D. Porter
Commanding N.A. Squadron, Flag-Ship Malvern.

P.S. I omitted to mention the capture of forty-four sick and wounded rebel soldiers, with the rebel surgeon and nurses in charge.

W.B. CUSHING

LAWS AND RESOLUTIONS
OF THE
STATE OF NORTH CAROLINA
PASSED BY THE
GENERAL ASSEMBLY
AT ITS
SESSION OF 1887,
BEGUN AND HELD IN THE CITY OF RALEIGH
ON WEDNESDAY, THE FIFTH DAY OF JANUARY, A.D. 1887,
TO WHICH ARE PREFIXED
A A REGISTER OF STATE OFFICERS, JUDICIARY,
A LIST OF COMMISSIONERS OF AFFIDAVITS,
MEMBERS OF THE GENERAL ASSEMBLY,
AND STATE CONSTITUTION.

PUBLISHED BY AUTHORITY

RALEIGH:
JOSEPHUS DANIELS, State Printer and Binder.
1887.

CHAPTER 76.

An act to amend the charter of the town of Smithville in Brunswick county, and to change the name thereof.

The General Assembly of North Carolina do enact:

SECTION 1. That the name of the town of Smithville, in the county of Brunswick, be changed to Southport.

SEC. 2. That the charter of the said town of Smithville, granted by the general assembly November fifteenth, seventeen hundred and ninety- two, and all acts of subsequent legislation respecting said town, be so amended as to erase the name of "Smithville," wherever it occurs in said charter or subsequent acts, and to insert Southport in lieu thereof.

SEC. 3. This act shall be in force from and after the date of its ratification.

In the general assembly read three times, and ratified this the 4th day of March, A. D. 1887.

MAYORS

Those who have served Smithville/Southport as Mayor since 1874

No complete record prior to 1874

Samuel Price	1874-1875	L. T. Yaskill	1927-1931
Dr. Walter C. Curtis	1875-1876	Price Furpless	1931-1935
	1876-	John D. Erikson	1935-1949
Philip Prioleau	1879-1880	H. A. Livingston	1949-1951
Rev. J. L. Keene	1880-1881	H. W. Hood	1951-1952
Lewis Jones	1881-1882	T. B. Carr	1952-1952
L. A. Galloway	1882-1884	J. A. Gilbert	1952-1955
D. I. Watson	-1892	Roy Robinson	1955-1957
R. M. Wescott	1892-1895	E. B. Tomlinson	1957-1959
E. H. Cranmer	1895-1900	Roy Robinson	1959-1961
Edward F. Gordon	1898-1900	J. E. Hahn	1961-1963
J. A. Williams	1900-1901	E. B. Tomlinson	1963-1971
Sam P. Swain	1901-1905	Lester V. Lowe	1971-1971
M. C. Guthrie	1905-1910	Dot Gilbert	1971-1973
Price Furpless	1910-1915	E. B. Tomlinson	1973-1983
J. W. Ruark	1915-1922	Norman R. Holden	1983-1989
T. B. Carr	1922-1925	C. B. Caroon	1989-1991
C. L. Stevens	1925-1927	Norman R. Holden	1991-

Compiled by Sylvia H. Butterworth, Financial Officer, City of Southport.

ORIGINAL LOT OWNERS

A public subscription was held in Wilmington on March 9, 1793, for the sale of the original 100 lots of the Town of Smithville. Some of the lots were not sold until later; deeds for some were never recorded or were lost during the Civil War when many court records were destroyed.

Ronald Gooding of Long Beach has done extensive research in the deed records and court minutes of Brunswick County as to the first lot owners. He has graciously given permission to use the research results in this book.

ORIGINAL LOT OWNERS AS DETERMINED BY LOTTERY AS ORDERED BY THE NORTH CAROLINA GENERAL ASSEMBLY IN NOVEMBER, 1792

LOT NO.	DRAWN NAME	VOL.	PAGE	NOTES
1	Robert Galloway	D	36-37	
2	Peter Harris	J	81	
3	Henry Long	D	75-76	
4	Henry Long	''	''	
5				
6	William E. Lord	D	4-6	
7	Thomas Flowers	D	65-66	
8	Henry Toomer	F	34-35	
9	Sarah Galloway	C	232-234	
10	John Brown	C	331-332	
11	Richard Parrish			No deed is indexed to Richard Parrish. Info deed Rich. Parrish to William Cook (D-1) 2/27/1795
12	Joseph Swain	E	20-21	
13	James Walker			See deed to Robert Wade (D-22) 12/16/1795

LOT NO.	DRAWN NAME	VOL.	PAGE	NOTES
14	Benjamin Smith	C	352-354	
15	William Gore *	''	''	Sold to Benjamin Smith
16	John Allen *	''	''	Sold to Benjamin Smith
17	William Dyer(?) * (Probably Dry)	D	72-73	Sold to Joshua Potts
18	William E. Lord	D	4-6	This lot was noted as being drawn for him but is not described in the body of the deed.
19	John Johnston	C	342-344	
20	Benjamin Smith	C	352-354	
21	William Campbell	H	70-72	
22	Solomon Hickman(?)	C	344-345	
23	Joshua Potts	D	72-73	
24				
25	Charles Crapton (?) Probably Crapon			No deed to Crapton. Info deed John Ralph to B.J. White (D-62/63). Refers to Crapton as original owner.
26	Charles Gause	D	6-8	
27				
28	William E. Lord	D	4-6	
29	Caleb Davis	D	41-42	
30	John McClellan	C	285-286	Error in deed. Deed reads, ''Lot 30 was drawn for John McAlister.''

LOT NO.	DRAWN NAME	VOL.	PAGE	NOTES
31	Henry Toomer	F	34-35	
32	Mary Jone Dry *	C	356-357	M.J. Dry to Nathan Warton. N. Warton to James White.
33	Robert Howe			No deed to Howe. Info deed from Howe to S. Russ (C-359)
34	Mary Jane Dry *	C	352-354	Sold to Benjamin Smith
35	Armond DeRosset	D	195	Also spelled DeRossett, Derossett, Derosett
36				
37	Elkanah Allen	D	73-74	
38	Henry Toomer	F	34-35	
39	James Parrish			No deed to Parrish. Info deed Parrish to Joseph Bunch (D-23) 3/11/1795
40	Jesie Potts	D	66-67	
41	John Gasper (?) *	E	20-21	Requit to Joseph Swain
42	Charles Gause	D	6-8	
43	James Parrish			No deed to Parrish. Info deed from Parrish to Wilson Davis (D-76/77)
44	Joseph Guatier	C	347-348	
45				
46				
47				

LOT NO.	DRAWN NAME	VOL.	PAGE	NOTES
48	Charles Crapton (?) Probably Crapon			No deed to Crapton. Info deed to J. Ralph to J. Potts on behalf his daughter Ann Eliza Potts (D-80)
49				
50	Henry Long, Sr.	D	75-76	
51	William H. McKenzie to Samuel Potter 1811	G	45	Then to Robert Potter in 1814; inherited by Rebecca Potter Drew.
52				
53	Benjamin Smith	C	352-354	
54				
55				
56				
57				
58				
59	Henry Long, Sr.	D	75-56	
60	William E. Lord	D	4-6	
61				
62	William E. Lord	D	4-6	
63	Jesse Potts	D	66-67	
64				
65	John Waddell *	C	352-354	Sold to Benjamin Smith
66	Mary Jane Dry *	C	352-354	Sold to Benjamin Smith
67				
68				
69				
70				
71				

LOT NO.	DRAWN NAME	VOL.	PAGE	NOTES
72				
73				
74				
75				
76	James Read	D	3-4	
77				
78	Joseph R. Gautier	C	347-348	
79	Benjamin Smith *	D	286-287	Relinquished to John Martin
80	John McKenzie *	H	125-128	Transferred to Robert Muter
81	Robert Muter	' '	' '	
82	William E. Lord	D	4-6	
83	Mary Jane Dry *	C	352-354	Sold to Benjamin Smith
84	John Waddell *	' '	' '	Sold to Benjamin Smith
85	Henry Toomer	F	34-35	
86	John Brown	C	331-332	
87	Robert Howe			No deed to Howe. Info deed from Howe to S. Russ (C-359)
88	James Read	D	3-4	
89	Charles Gause	D	6-8	
90	John Johnston	C	342-344	
91				
92	Thomas Flowers	D	65-66	
93	Joshua Potts	D	72-73	
94	John Johnston	C	342-344	
95	John Wilkinson (?)			No deed to Wilkinson. His name was shown as an adjoiner in another deed.
96	William Campbell	H	70-72	

LOT NO.	DRAWN NAME	VOL.	PAGE	NOTES
97	Henry Toomer	F	34-35	
98	Charles Gause	D	6-8	
99	Joshua Potts	D	72-73	
100	Henry Toomer	F	34-35	

* = Name drawn but did not purchase lot(s). Instead sold or re-leased to other party.

Compiled by R.L. Gooding in 1991.

RATES OF PILOTAGE

For the Cape Fear Bars and River,
established on the 18th day of September, 1868,
in accordance with existing Acts of the Legislature of North Carolina.

BARS.

Every vessel drawing six				feet water and under seven				feet	....	$ 9 00
"	"	"	seven	"	"	"	"	eight	"	....	10 75
"	"	"	eight	"	"	"	"	nine	"	....	12 00
"	"	"	nine	"	"	"	"	ten	"	....	13 50
"	"	"	ten	"	"	"	"	eleven	"	....	15 25
"	"	"	eleven	"	"	"	"	twelve	"	....	18 50
"	"	"	twelve	"	"	"	"	thirteen	"	....	22 50
"	"	"	thirteen	"	"	"	"	fourteen	"	....	28 50
"	"	"	fourteen	"	"	"	"	fifteen	"	....	34 00
"	"	"	sixteen	"	"	"	over	....	45 00

RIVER.

										From Smithville to Wilmington and vice versa.	From Five Fathom Hole to Wilmington and vice versa.
Every vessel drawing six				feet water and under seven				feet	......	$ 9 50	$ 7.00
"	"	"	seven	"	"	"	"	eight	"	......	12 00	9.00
"	"	"	eight	"	"	"	"	nine	"	......	13 00	10 25
"	"	"	nine	"	"	"	"	ten	"	......	14 00	11 25
"	"	"	ten	"	"	"	"	eleven	"	......	15 00	13 25
"	"	"	eleven	"	"	"	"	twelve	"	......	19 75	15 75
"	"	"	twelve	"	"	"	"	thirteen	"	......	24 00	17 50
"	"	"	thirteen	"	"	"	"	fourteen	"	......	29 00	22 25
"	"	"	fourteen	"	"	"	"	fifteen	"	......	35 00	26 25
"	"	"	fifteen	"	"	"	"	sixteen	"	......	44 00	30 00
"	"	"	sixteen	"	"	"	over	....	46 00	33 00

From Smithville to Brunswick, or from Brunwick to Wilmington or VICE VER-
SA, shall be one-half the pilotage from Smithville to Wilmington. From
Smithville to Five Fathom Hole, from Five Fathom Hole to Brunswick, from
Brunswick to Campbell's Island, from Campbell's Island to Wilmington or VICE
VERSA, one-fourth of the pilotage from Smithville to Wilmington. *Provided*,
That vessels of 60 tons birthen, owned by citizens of this State, shall not be
required to take a pilot.

By order,

B. J. LAWTON, Clerk, B.C.

SEPTEMBER 18, 1868

Journal Steam Power Press Print, Wilmington, N. C.

RAILROAD CELEBRATION
Southport, N.C. November 23, 1911
11 O'Clock A.M.

P R O G R A M

PRESIDENT Z. W. WHITEHEAD, MASTER OF CEREMONIES

Song . . . . America
Prayer . . . . K. B. Tupper, D. D., L. L. D.
Welcome Address. . . . . Robert W. Davis, Esq.
Response . . . . J. D. Smith, Mayor of Wilmington, N. C.
Address . . . . Representative H. L. Godwin
Address . . . . George Rountree, Esq.
Address. . . . . Harry Skinner, Esq.
Address. . . . . J. O. Carr, Esq.
Address . . . . Senator Lee S. Overman
Address . . . . Senator F. M. Simmons
Address . . . . His Excellency Gov. W. W. Kitchin
  Appreciative gift from the citizens of Brunswick county to
  President Z. W. Whitehead. . . . .
  . . . . Presentation by C. Ed. Taylor, Esq.
1:30 P.M. picnic dinner and barbecue in Franklin Square.
2:30 P.M., motor boat parade in harbor viewed from Garrison.
3:00 P. M., field sports in Franklin Square:
  100 yard dash for State championship.
  High jump.
  Bayonet drill by soldiers from Fort Caswell.
  Tug of war—Fort Caswell vs. Southport.
  Relay race.
  Bag race.
  Light calisthenics by U. S. soldiers.
Music during the day by military band from Fort Caswell.
  The Steamer General G. W. Getty will make regular trips to and
from Fort Caswell during the afternoon for the acommodation of
visitors.

Bibliography
and
Suggested Reading List

Battle, Kemp P., ed. *Letters and Documents, Relating to the Early History of the Lower Cape Fear* (James Sprunt Historical Monograph No. 4). Chapel Hill: The University of North Carolina Press, 1903.

Bennett, Charles E. and Lennon, Donald R. *A Quest for Glory*. Chapel Hill: The University of North Carolina Press, 1991.

Bentley, Joseph H. *Fort Johnston in the History of the Lower Cape Fear*. Typescript, 1970.

Bowen, Catherine Drinker. *The Miracle at Philadelphia: The Story of the Constitutional Convention*. Boston: Little, Brown & Co., 1966.

Butler, Lindley S. and Watson, Alan D. *The North Carolina Experience, An Interpretive and Documentary History*. Chapel Hill: The University of North Carolina Press, 1984.

Cashman, Dianne Cobb. *Cape Fear Adventure*. Woodland Hills, CA: Windsor Publications, 1982.

Cashman, Dianne Cobb. *Headstrong: The Biography of Amy Morris Bradley, 1823-1904*. Wilmington, NC: Broadfoot Publishing Co., 1990.

Carson, Susan C. *By Faith We Serve*. Southport, NC: Southport Baptist Church, 1981.

Clark, Walter, ed. *Colonial and State Records of North Carolina* (16 volumes). Winston-Salem and Winston-Salem and Goldsboro, NC: State of North Carolina, 1895-1906.

Corbitt, David Leroy. *Explorations, Descriptions, and Attempted Settlements of Carolina, 1584-1590*. Raleigh: Division of Archives and History, 1952.

Crittenden, Charles C. *The Commerce of North Carolina, 1763-1789.* New Haven: Yale University Press, 1937.

Curtis, Margaret. *Diary: 1886-1896.* Unpublished.

Curtis, W.G. *Reminiscences of Smithville and Wilmington (1848-1900).* Private publishing.

Davis, Kenneth C. *Don't Know Much About History.* New York: Avon Books, 1991.

Evans, W. McKee. *Ballots and Fence Rails: Reconstruction on Lower Cape Fear.* Chapel Hill: The University of North Carolina Press, 1966.

Flexner, James Thomas. *Washington, The Indispensable Man.* Boston: Little, Brown & Co., 1969.

Graves, Mae Blake. *Land Grants of New Hanover County.* Wilmington, NC: 1980.

Hale, Judson. *The Best of The Old Farmer's Almanac.* New York: Random House, 1991.

Herring, Ethel. *Cap'n Charlie and the Lights of the Lower Cape Fear.* Winston-Salem, NC: Hunter Publishing Company, 1967.

Herring, Ethel and Williams, Carolee. *Fort Caswell in War and Peace.* Wendell, NC: Broadfoot's Bookmark, 1983.

Holden, J.M.M. *Heartening Heritage On a Carolina Crescent.* Wilmington, NC: New Hanover Printing and Publishing Co., 1989.

Lawson, John. *Lawson's History of North Carolina.* Richmond, VA: Garrett & Massie Publishers, 1951.

Lee, E. Lawrence. *The History of Brunswick County, North Carolina.* Brunswick County Board of Commissioners, 1976.

Lee, E. Lawrence. *The Lower Cape Fear in Colonial Days.* Chapel Hill: The University of North Carolina Press, 1965.

Lee, Robert E. *Blackbeard the Pirate.* Winston-Salem, NC: John F. Blair, 1974.

Lefler, Hugh T. *The History of a Southern State: North Carolina.* Chapel Hill: The University of North Carolina Press, 1954.

Lemmon, Sarah McCulloh. *North Carolina's Role in the First World War*. Raleigh: Division of Archives and History, 1975.

Lemmon, Sarah McCulloh. *North Carolina's Role in World War II*. Raleigh: Division of Archives and History, 1964.

Lennon, Donald R. and Kellum, Ida Brooks. *The Wilmington Town Book (1743-1778)*. Raleigh: Division of Archives and History, 1973.

Lounsbury, Carl. *The Architecture of Southport*. Southport, NC: Southport Historical Society, 1979.

McKoy, Elizabeth Francenia. *Early Wilmington, Block by Block*. Raleigh: Edwards & Broughton Co., 1967.

Morison, Samuel Eliot. *The European Discovery of America, The Southern Voyages*. Oxford University Press, 1974.

Parker, Mattie Erma Edwards. *N.C. Charters and Constitutions, 1578-1698*. Raleigh: Carolina Charter Tercentenary Commission, 1963.

Pendered, Norman C. *Stede Bonnet, Gentleman Pirate*. Manteo, NC: Times Printing Company, Inc., 1977.

Ross, Malcolm. *The Cape Fear* (Part of the "Rivers of America" series). New York: Holt, Rinehart and Winston, Inc., 1965.

Ruark, Robert. *The Old Man and the Boy*. New York: Henry Holt and Co., 1953.

Ruark, Robert. *The Old Man's Boy Grows Older*. New York: Holt, Rinehart and Winston, Inc., 1957.

Schaw, Janet. *Journal of a Lady of Quality: Being the Narrative of a Journey from Scotland to the West Indies, North Carolina, and Portugal, in the Years, 1774 to 1776*. Edited by Evangeline W. Andrews in collaboration with Charles M. Andrews. New Haven: Yale University Press, 1923.

Schlereth, Thomas J. *Victorian America*. New York: Harper Collins, 1991.

Schmidt, Dorcas W. *The Cemeteries of Southport and Surrounding Area*. Southport, NC: Southport Historical Society, 1983.

Sprunt, James. *Chronicles of the Cape Fear River*. Reprinted by Reprint Company of Spartanburg, SC, 1973.

Sprunt, James. *Tales and Traditions of the Lower Cape Fear*. Reprinted by the Reprint Company of Spartanburg, SC, 1973.

Stick, David. *Bald Head Island*. Wendell, NC: Broadfoot Publishers, 1985.

Stick, David. *North Carolina Lighthouses*. Raleigh: North Carolina Department of Cultural Resources, 1982.

Watson, Alan D., Lawson, Dennis R. and Lennon, Donald R. *Harnett, Hooper, and Howe, Revolutionary Leaders of the Lower Cape Fear*. Wilmington, NC: Lower Cape Fear Historical Society, Inc., 1979.

Williams, Isabel and McEachern, Leora. *Salt—That Necessary Article*. Wilmington, NC: Louis Toomer Moore Memorial Fund, 1973.

Wise, Stephen R. *Lifeline of the Confederacy*. Columbia, SC: University of South Carolina Press, 1988.

Also consulted were the Brunswick County records (marriages, deaths, court minutes, censuses, etc.) on microfilm, and newspapers on microfilm. Personal interviews, letters and scrapbooks used were from Minnie F. Kotowski, Mary L. McKeithan, Edward Jelks, Lucy Avant, Elnora Rogers, Wanda Golden, Trudy Hufham, Sally McNeil, and Thelma S. Dunn.

INDEX

165

166

167